CU00767054

Samuel L. Kimbles (doctor brother man), my dear friend and colleague, is one of the kindest, most compassionate intellectuals that I know. In this time of national crisis precipitated by the COVID-19 pandemic and the relentless violence against Black, Brown, and Indigenous bodies, Sam's latest book, *Intergenerational Complexes in Analytical Psychology: The Suffering of Ghosts*, provides a psychoanalytic lens to illustrate our complicity in past traumatic cultural histories and contemporary injustices. In his brilliant, insightful analysis, Sam focuses on how we use our own personal suffering as a defense against recognizing the ways in which we are implicated in the suffering of others. As such, we miss opportunities for the mutual recognition essential for reparative communication and instead, both consciously and unconsciously, perpetuate social enactments that replicate intergenerational traumatic cultural experiences in our current everyday lives. I strongly recommend this book for anyone who is interested in understanding the psychosocial underpinnings of our ongoing cultural strife and who believes that insight can lead to behavioral change. *Intergenerational Complexes in Analytical Psychology* lights a pathway for a brighter collective future.

— **Medria L. Connolly**, *PhD, co-author with Bryan K. Nichols of*
Transforming Ghosts into Ancestors: Un-silencing the
Psychological Case for Reparations to Descendants
of American Slavery

Sam Kimbles has once again substantially deepened our understanding of how unconscious dynamics operate in political, social, and cultural and group processes. In this book, he pulls together histories of violence, oppression, and social injustices to present to the reader an emotional field in which psyche generates its own responses and creates conditions for subjectivity grounded in the cultural unconscious. On such a reading of the psyche, we see in a remarkably rich and attuned way what possibilities exist for change and healing. Sam's work represents a significant contribution to our field.

— **Andrew Samuels**, *former Professor of Analytical Psychology,
University of Essex, and author of* The Political Psyche

If your ghosts were stolen from Africa, sold into slavery, or were indigenous peoples deprived of their lands, or immigrants fleeing poverty, famine, and war, or Jewish refugees from the Nazis, Central American refugees from gangs, all of you have terrible stories to tell. How do those of us who work with human suffering treat your pain? How do we heal the severed feeling of kinship in our culture, our recognition of each other as fellow citizens, all of us carriers of ancestral trauma? These are among the questions Samuel Kimbles addresses in his wise and compassionate book. . . . *Intergenerational Complexes in Analytical Psychology* is a major contribution to Jungian thought, a profound and hopeful call to bring what Jungians know about working with the unconscious into the social and cultural realm. If your ghosts are agitated, moaning and muttering, rolling over in their graves, read them this book. They will thank you for it.

— **Naomi Ruth Lowinsky**, *author of* The Rabbi, the Goddess and Jung: Getting the Word from Within

Intergenerational Complexes in Analytical Psychology

Intergenerational Complexes in Analytical Psychology: The Suffering of Ghosts draws attention to human suffering and how it relates to unacknowledged and unrecognized traumatic cultural histories that continue to haunt us in the present. The book shows the many ways that our internal lives are organized and patterned by both racial, ethnic, and national identities, and personal experiences.

This book shows how the cultural unconscious with its multiple group dynamics, identities, nationalities, seething differences of conflicts, polarizations, and individual personalities are organized by cultural complexes and narrated by archetypal story formations, which the author calls phantom narratives. The emotional dynamics generated constitute potential transitional spaces or holding containers that allow us to work with these issues psychologically at both the individual and group levels, offering opportunities for healing. The chapters of the book provide numerous examples of the applications of these terms to natural and cultural catastrophes as well as expressions as uncanny phenomena.

Intergenerational Complexes in Analytical Psychology is essential reading for analytical psychologists, Jungian psychotherapists, and other professionals seeking to understand the impact of intergenerational trauma on individuals and groups. It is also relevant to the work of academics and scholars of Jungian studies, sociology, trauma studies, politics, and social justice.

Samuel L. Kimbles is a psychologist, Jungian analyst, member and former president of the C. G. Jung Institute of San Francisco, and a clinical professor (VCF) in the Department of Family and Community Medicine at the University of California, San Francisco. He has a private practice in San Francisco and Santa Rosa, California, and works as a clinical consultant to organizations. In addition to lecturing and presenting widely, he has published several works on the cultural complex. *Phantom Narratives: The Unseen Contributions of Culture to Psyche* explores the themes of psyche in groups and society. This book, *Intergenerational Complexes in Analytical Psychology: The Suffering of Ghosts*, continues the processes of exploring the unconscious at the level of culture and groups.

Intergenerational Complexes in Analytical Psychology

The Suffering of Ghosts

Samuel L. Kimbles

Routledge
Taylor & Francis Group

LONDON AND NEW YORK

First published 2021
by Routledge
2 Park Square, Milton Park, Abingdon, Oxon OX14 4RN

and by Routledge
605 Third Avenue, New York, NY 10158

*Routledge is an imprint of the Taylor & Francis Group, an
informa business*

British Library Cataloguing-in-Publication Data
A catalogue record for this book is available from the
British Library

Library of Congress Cataloging-in-Publication Data
Names: Kimbles, Samuel L., author.
Title: Intergenerational complexes in analytical psychology :
    the suffering of ghosts / Samuel L. Kimbles.
Description: Abingdon, Oxon ; New York, NY : Routledge,
    2021. | Includes bibliographical references and index.
Identifiers: LCCN 2020049096 (print) | LCCN 2020049097
    (ebook) | ISBN 9780367513221 (hbk) | ISBN 9780367513269
    (pbk) | ISBN 9781003053378 (ebk)
Subjects: LCSH: Intergroup relations. | Jungian psychology. |
    Intergenerational relations—Psychological aspects. | Social
    conflict—Psychological aspects.
Classification: LCC HM716 .K55 2021 (print) | LCC HM716
    (ebook) | DDC 302.3—dc23
LC record available at https://lccn.loc.gov/2020049096
LC ebook record available at https://lccn.loc.gov/2020049097

ISBN: 978-0-367-51322-1 (hbk)
ISBN: 978-0-367-51326-9 (pbk)
ISBN: 978-1-003-05337-8 (ebk)

Typeset in Times New Roman
by Apex CoVantage, LLC

To my father and mother, Nelson and Margaret (Maggie) Kimbles, from whom I learned about the lineage that then opened the doors to the ancestors.

Those who know ghosts tell us that they long to be released from their ghost life and led to rest as ancestors. As ancestors, they live forth in the present generation, while as ghosts they are compelled to haunt the present generation with their shadow life.

H. W. Loewald, "On the Therapeutic Action of Psycho-Analysis"

Contents

Foreword

If your ghosts were stolen from Africa, sold into slavery, or were indigenous peoples deprived of their lands, or immigrants fleeing poverty, famine, and war, or Jewish refugees from the Nazis, or Central American refugees from gangs, all of you have terrible stories to tell. How do those of us who work with human suffering treat your pain? How do we heal the severed feeling of kinship in our culture, our recognition of each other as fellow citizens, all of us carriers of ancestral trauma? These are among the questions Samuel L. Kimbles addresses in his wise and compassionate book. He seeks the healing of our cultural agony, reminding us that we are bound to each other.

Kimbles confronts the Tower of Babel that dominates our cultural landscape, full of competing assumptions and ideologies, where ghosts from different lineages argue with one another about who is suffering more and no one can understand the other. This Tower of Babel is a cultural complex, signifying the "cold civil war that never ends." Kimbles argues, as he has for many years and in many books, that Jungian psychology needs to address the social reality of people's lives and the cultural level of the psyche. What's missing in all the chaos and fury of our times is a psychological attitude. He invites us and our suffering ghosts into a safe space, where our ghosts can hear each other's stories, remember our shared history. "Each subgroup is carrying a shard of the cultural vessel," he writes, referring to the Jewish mystical idea of "Tikkun Olam," healing the world.

Intergenerational Complexes in Analytical Psychology: The Suffering of Ghosts is a major contribution to Jungian thought, a profound and hopeful call to bring what Jungians know about working with the unconscious into the social and cultural realm. If your ghosts are agitated, moaning and muttering, rolling over in their graves, read them this book. They will thank you for it.

Naomi Ruth Lowinsky
Author of *The Rabbi, the Goddess and Jung:
Getting the Word from Within*

Preface

As expressions of normative unconsciousness, psychodynamic treatments, in general, and traditional psychoanalysis, in particular, are the products of European and American cultural socialization, which emphasizes autonomy, individuality, freedom, purity, and the denial of whiteness as privilege and power. Thus, there tends to be unconsciousness about how this acculturation contributes to our theories, clinical work, and the understanding of emotional suffering. Our theories are not as racially or culturally free of the bias of cultural complexes as they may seem to imply. What Jung stated in 1946 applies equally to our current times:

> We are living in times of great disruption: political passions are aflame, internal upheavals have brought nations to the brink of chaos, and the very foundations of our *Weltanschauung* are shattered. This critical state of things has such a tremendous influence on the psychic life of the individual that the doctor must follow its effects with more than usual attention. The storm of events does not sweep down upon him only from the great world outside; he feels the violence of its impact even in the quiet of his consulting room. . . . As he has a responsibility towards his patients, he cannot afford to withdraw to the peaceful island of undisturbed scientific work, but must descend into the arena of world events, in order to join in the battle of conflicting passions and opinions. Were he to remain aloof from the tumult, the calamity of his time would reach him only from afar, and the patients suffering would find neither ear nor understanding. He would be at a loss to know how to talk to him, and to help him out of his isolation . . . the psychologist cannot avoid coming to grips with contemporary history, even if his very soul shrinks from the political uproar, the lying propaganda, and the jarring speeches of the demagogues. We need not mention his duties as a citizen, which confronts him with a similar task.
>
> (Jung, 1968, pp. 177–178)

We are living in an historical moment similar to that described by Jung during World War II. We have not created a space for social and political processes to be theorized as significant psychodynamic factors that affect our subjectivity, especially for those marginalized by racial, cultural, gender, and sexual traumas. And "what is less focused on is an acknowledgment and articulation of the layer within the psyche that contains and secrets crimes against humanity and their history" (Holmes, 2016, p. 642).

In addition to the dominant themes in European and American socialization just mentioned, the emotional and cultural fallout from conditions created for nonwhites revolve around feelings of being silenced, unseen, unheard, invisible, nameless, and marginalized. These feelings reflect responses to social and political contexts that function within an aspirational framework, such as "equal justice under the law" or "all men are created equal" on the one hand and the evidence of structural racism (disparities in healthcare, education, income) on the other. Though the dominant analytic orientations have remained intrapsychic and, of late, relational, the cultural attitudes implicit in psychological work have been similarly marginalized, thus haunting not only our cultural behavior but also our psychological work. The relational models, although they create more conceptual space for the sociocultural dimensions of this larger context, have been slow to evolve.

Intergenerational Complexes in Analytical Psychology: The Suffering of Ghosts is also, of course, my way of calling attention to the unacknowledged, unprocessed consequences of group traumas (violence) that I have personally seen reappear over and over again because of social and political violence around differences of race, class, gender, and sexual orientations. These histories and their various sociopolitical contexts are phantomatic for me in the sense that they constitute previously unacknowledged stories – and sometimes unimagined histories that generated stories I needed to listen to – that, as I retell them, will, I believe, affect others through their telling presence in our socioemotional environment that we all share.

My approach to these themes and issues uses both the practice and the lens of Jung's analytical psychology. As an analyst, I have long marveled at the role of cultural consciousness in contextualizing some of our deepest personal experiences, and I have learned that attention to social reality deeply influences the psychological well-being of the individual self. As someone often consulted by people who want to restore their effective participation in life, I have found that such essential human senses as agency, choice, and the ability to locate ourselves and hold our own within societal structures only emerge when the psychic consequences of feeling separate from others are adequately explored.

This book contains a number of my papers, some previously published, others presented at professional meetings. Together, they show my continued dreaming forward the concept of the cultural complex, of phantoms, phantomatic complexes, and phantom narratives to locate the collective dreams, fantasies, and imaginative reconstruction of historical complexes that, however intergenerational, are pressing for present-day integration and resolution. The past four-hundred-plus years in relationship to slavery and the genocidal destruction of millions of indigenous people here in the United States have been the open secret of our unacknowledged violence.

An old Bushman saying – "there is a dream, dreaming us" – has been the primal ground leading me into and through the historical nightmares that fill our newspapers today. Even natural catastrophes (hurricanes, tsunamis) seem to flush out of the swamp of cultural complexes many culturally imposed traumas (see Chapter 2). These issues are so ubiquitous partially due to their structural forms, for instance, structural racism. We don't see that we swim together in these turbulent cultural waters and are affected by and contribute to their disturbances, consciously and unconsciously. Othering and demonizing differences are expressions of part of the structure of cultural complexes and are used to justify and deny our positions in what we are creating.

The line between what is clinical and what is not needs to be crossed to include issues of injustice, structural racism, and our own contributions to these cultural traumas, not only countertransferentially, but also as citizens of and in the very institutions that foster unhealthy context for us all. For the suffering ghosts that haunt us are "not simply a dead or missing person, but a social figure, and investigating it can lead to that dense site where history and subjectivity make social life" (Gordon, 2008, p. 8).

The reader can follow my thinking and attitude of making space for us to stand as we enter these complex and chaotic times in this our cultural and global moment. This attitude requires us to sit with uncertainty, to bear conscious witness, to be engaged citizens, to live in the spaces of our differences and rework the links that connect us. This evolving attitude will, I believe, help us to develop our capacities to work toward a wholeness of psyche and culture. The chapters in this book give many ways that ghostly processes are manifested in our social and political lives, offering opportunities for potential healing of our cultural complexes.

References

Gordon, A. (2008). *Ghostly matters: Haunting and the sociological imagination.* Minneapolis, MN: University of Minnesota Press.

Holmes, D. E. (2016). Culturally imposed trauma: The sleeping dog has awakened. Will psychoanalysis take head? *Psychoanalytic Dialogues, 26*(6), 641–654.

Jung, C. G. (1968). Preface to essays on contemporary events. In W. McGuire (Ed.), *The collected works of C.G. Jung: Vol. 10. Civilization in transition.* Princeton, NJ: Princeton University Press.

Acknowledgments

This book grew out of my ongoing engagements with many friends, colleagues, patients, institutions, and friends. It builds upon many encounters with groups, with psychotherapy and medical care, with and within organizations. Throughout my professional life, my focus has been on the individual and the group – the living contexts of our lives: the family, social systems of all sorts, as well as cultural and political processes. I had the benefit of generous support and input from many along the way, those who heard and helped me to see the implications of my thinking and feeling through providing patience and good humor.

For a twenty-year period, Suzy Spradlin, analyst and friend, and I trained various groups of psychoanalysts from all over the country to learn to work with the unconscious at the level of the group. This work gave me a visceral feel for how the unconscious at the level of the group moves and shapes subjectivity and intersubjectivity. I also appreciate the ongoing support of my consultants, Tom Ogden and John Beebe.

So many friends and colleagues have offered years of sustenance: Medria Connolly and I have been in regular communication over the years about things cultural. Naomi Lowinsky and Dan Safran's continual support around these issues, especially transgenerational processes, have proven invaluable. Ritch Addison and I, as faculty members of the Family and Community Residency program, taught, consulted, and led weekly professional and development groups for over thirty years. Jeff Swanger, Mark Sullivan, and Paul Fishman helped me create a place wherein we could make sense of the personal and institutional dynamics of our own San Francisco C. G. Jung Institute. These ongoing conversations kept present and alive the unconscious in group life in which we were members.

To the staff, clinicians, and youths who provided a space for my ongoing consultations to TLC Child and Family Services, and the lives of hundreds of young people over a thirty-year period, thank you.

To my dear wife, Sara, who always has been an ear and an open heart when I needed to make personal sense of all that I was carrying. The creativity and love in her responses brought color and smiles to my life.

To my family, who provided holding and containing for the deeply personal side of my living. To mix a metaphor, living with cultural complexes is not like a soft sleeping pillow. There are edges, bumps on the journey. "Stony is the Road." All the while I was being transformed in ways that I later discovered.

To the many who sacrificed their lives before me in the name of Freedom and Justice for all. Their spirits gave me needed wisdom and support.

Stony the Road we trod,
Bitter the Chast'ning rod
Felt in days when hope
Unborn had died

From James Weldon Johnson,
Lift Every Voice and Sing
The Negro National Anthem, 1900

Credits

"My Great Grandfather's Slaves." Copyright © 2012 by Wendell Berry from *New Collected Poems*. Reprinted by permission of Counterpoint Press.

"Phantom Narratives and the Uncanny in Cultural Life: Psychic Presences and Their Shadows," by Samuel Kimbles, *The European Journal of Psychotherapy and Counselling, 18*(6). Reprinted by permission of Taylor & Francis, Ltd. (www.tandfonline.com).

"A Framework for Cultural Activism in the Consulting Room," by Samuel Kimbles, in *Analysis and Activism: Social and Political Contributions of Jungian Psychology*, edited by Emilija Kiehl, Mark Saban, and Andrew Samuels. Routledge, 2016. Reprinted by permission of the publisher.

Excerpt(s) from *Fences* by August Wilson, copyright © 1986 by August Wilson. Used by permission of New American Library, an imprint of Penguin Publishing Group, a division of Penguin Random House LLC. All rights reserved.

"James Baldwin and Toni Morrison: Othering through Racialized Intersubjectivities," by Samuel Kimbles, *Jung Journal: Culture & Psyche, 14*(3). Reprinted by permission of Taylor & Francis, Ltd. (www.tandfonline.com).

Introduction

We are the ones, we are the ones, and we've been waiting . . .
We are the ones we've been waiting . . .
We are the ones; we've been waiting for . . .
We are, the one, we've been waiting for . . .

Sweet Honey in the Rocks

The invisible see us.
The forgotten recall us.
When we see ourselves we see them
When we turn away, do they?

Eduardo Galeano

What does it mean to wake up into transitional spaces? Can the cultural unconscious with its multiple group dynamics, seething differences of conflicts, polarizations, individual personalities and its cultural complexes constitute such a transitional space? A holding container? How do we work with the suffering and pain caused by group polarizations, violence, and hate? After many generations of heroic struggles to overcome psychic hardships associated with differences created by allegiances to religious, political, and identity groups, what can we do with our experiences of betrayal, disillusionment, and loss in being with each other? How do we process and make sense of our many reactions, thoughts, emotions, and impulses triggered by being with each other's intergenerational traumas, given the historization of their and our subjectivities? In other words, how we are made by and how do we make ourselves out of our conscious and unconscious histories? How are we implicated and related to each other's suffering? The aforementioned dynamics have produced alternative narratives for our identity groups, producing different social and political agendas and realities.

Intergenerational Complexes in Analytical Psychology: The Suffering of Ghosts draws attention to human suffering and how it relates to unacknowledged and unrecognized traumatic cultural histories that continue to haunt us in the present. Seemingly, when we do recognize our own suffering, we tend to deny our complicity in the suffering of others. Through this separation into, as Jessica Benjamin (2006) describes, "doer and done to," we create situations of what I see as intersubjectives that generate cultural violence – the other becomes an object. The failure to recognize the other as a subject with a center of being with his or her own subjectivity represents a breakdown in the mutual recognition that forms the bedrock of an ethical and moral attitude for potential reparative efforts. Breakdowns in recognition create ruptures in the social fabric. Though the causes of these ruptures may be related to past harms and transgressions, they continue to be presences in our daily lives as representations of our intergenerational histories. These dynamics occur at every level of our emotional lives both at the conscious and unconscious levels.

At the level of the unconscious, certain kinds of images (*phantoms*) and affects that appear in the aftermath of natural and social catastrophes are representations of unconscious narratives (*phantom narratives*) expressing the inner psychological dimensions of culture's working interiority. These phantoms come with an underlying narrative structure, which I have previously described as *phantom narratives*, which show how the unconscious, working at the group and individual levels, provides intergenerational, political, and social contexts within which both individuals and groups may find a different kind of emotional containment for these catastrophes. In this way suffering may be potentially processed psychologically and related to symbolically.

In a conversation between James Hillman and Sonu Shamdasani, which was recorded in their book *Lament of the Dead* (2013), Hillman refers to an Egyptian practice of "opening the mouth of the dead." This metaphor was a way to open up *The Red Book*, where through Jung's descent into the underworld, he found a way to relate to the dead. *Intergenerational Complexes in Analytical Psychology: The Suffering of Ghosts* is my way of opening up cultural, social, and political life to the liminality of the unconscious dimension through which we experience and live out the patterns of our lives.

Aristotle states that we are social animals who associate to meet human needs. In the context of creating and fighting over social structures, these animal needs create the ongoing rubs expressed in Schopenhauer's image of humans being like porcupines who gather together for warmth but who must stay away from each other lest they prick and hurt each other. This tension in human relating is what has to be borne and worked with for group development to evolve. This level of group development means at the very least holding differences with minimal retaliation. The incarnation of the group as a factor in relating requires that we understand its dynamics so its actualization as a positive holding container may develop toward our ideals, as in "all men are created equal." This aspiration requires a level of emotional development at both the individual and the group level to actualize it as destiny.

I have spent many years working as a psychologist and psychoanalyst and as a consultant to groups and organizations in which the tension of being together rapidly regresses to splitting, blaming, attacking, and scapegoating. In an earlier paper, "The Myth of Invisibility," I introduced the concept of cultural complexes to show how cultural stereotypes expressed through unacknowledged racism rendered invisible those human beings who are the objects of such attitudes as well as the activity of cultural complexes that rendered those caught up within them invisible to themselves. I used Ralph Ellison's 1952 novel *Invisible Man* as a frame. It gives a dramatic illustration of this invisibility making dynamics active in structural but unconscious racism. The blindness made by cultural stereotypes and connected to racism gives rise to a deep and painful intrasubjectivity developed around finding a way to deal with the racial cultural complexes through working with one's internalized invisibility in the context of the culturally sanctioned damage done to one's being. The protagonist in Ellison's novel is a nameless African American man whom others are unable to see as he truly is, although he is "a man of substance, of flesh and bone, fiber and liquids – and I might even be said to possess a mind" (Ellison, 1952, p. 3). Instead, they perceive and engage a phantom of their own subconscious. Rather than interacting with him as an individual with personal aspirations and motivations, he is viewed as a stereotype, as an incarnation of an idea, a proxy for an assumed understanding of all African American men. "When they approach me they see only my surrounding, themselves, or figments of their imagination – indeed, everything and anything except me" (p. 3). Thus, through the stereotypical perspectives held by others, Ellison displays the individual personhood of an African American man rendered invisible through social and cultural attitudes.

Ellison portrays the struggles with becoming a self, finding identity and social equality in American society. In this sense we can paraphrase Jung, when he indicated the origins of subjectivity takes place in that "dense" underbrush where psyche and the social origins of the self converge and emerge. As Avery Gordon states, "it is an enchanted encounter in a disenchanted world between familiarity and estrangement" (2008, pp. 54–55):

> The ghost is not simply a dead or missing person but a social figure, and investigating it can lead to that dense site where history and subjectivity make social life. . . . The past *always* haunts the present [because the] forced "disappearance" of aspects of the social continues to shadow all that remains.
>
> (2008, pp. x, viii)

Cultural complex dynamics allow us to see and experience the internal dynamics of culture's working interiority. Phantom narratives build on a description introduced in Jung's paper on complex theory wherein he says,

> It [complex] is the image of a certain psychic situation which is strongly accentuated emotionally and is, moreover, incompatible with the habitual attitude of consciousness. This image has a powerful inner coherence, it has its own wholeness and, in addition, a relatively high degree of autonomy.
>
> (Jung, 1969, para. 201)

The psychic situations I am describing are the activities at the level of the cultural unconscious expressed as cultural complexes that provide coherence, autonomy, and emotional activation in the context of historicized narratives. By *historicized* I mean the cultural, historical, and present context that give rise to transgenerational complexes that bring past and present together within a current sociopolitical context. The cultural past brings with it ghosts that represent the unacknowledged harm done through violence to the selves of the exploited, denigrated, and colonized other.

To get to an acknowledging and working-through space requires that we understand and form a relationship with the psyche. Again, Jung says it:

> We need more understanding of human nature, because the only real danger that exists is man himself. He is the great danger, and we are pitifully unaware of it. We know nothing of man, far too little. His psyche should be studied, because we are the origin of all coming evil.
>
> (1977, p. 436)

I hear Jung speaking about the need to recognize, connect with, relate to the reality of the psyche as the starting point when we speak about change at whatever level.

Psychoanalyst Jeffrey Prager makes this point again:

> Yet racism inhabits the mind; it continues to possess a psychic reality all its own. It operates internally according to its own rules and logic. It remains in place and enacted in part because specific mechanisms required to loosen it have remained unconsciously repressed.
>
> (Prager, 2017, p. 2)

References

Benjamin, J. (2006). Two-way streets: Recognition of difference and the inter-subjective third. *Differences*, *17*, 116–146.

Ellison, R. (1952). *Invisible man*. New York, NY: Random House.

Gordon, A. (2008). *Ghostly matters: Haunting and the sociological imagination*. Minneapolis, MN: University of Minnesota Press.

Hillman, J., & Shamdasani, S. (2013). *Lament of the dead*. New York, NY: W.W. Norton & Company.

Jung, C. G. (1969). A review of the complex theory. In W. McGuire (Ed.), *The complete works of C.G. Jung: Vol. 8. The structure and dynamics of the psyche*. Princeton, NJ: Princeton University Press.

Jung, C. G. (1977). *C.G. Jung speaking*. Princeton, NJ: Princeton University Press.

Prager, J. (2017). Do Black lives matter? A psychoanalytic exploration of racism and American resistance to reparations. *Political Psychology*, *38*, 637–651. https://doi.org/10.1111/pops.12436 10.1111/pops.12436

Chapter 1

Working with cultural phantoms through cultural complexes

Recently, I saw the movie *Beasts of the Southern Wild* (Zeitlin, 2012) on a recommendation from friends who knew I was going to New Orleans for a conference. I thought the movie was fantastic, full of magical, imaginative, and gritty suffering, and the shadow associated with earthiness. I felt a type of immediacy as well as a separateness. It reminded me of Du Bois's image of the Veil, the kind of double consciousness that creates a barrier and a separation from otherness, making for an inner space. I also thought of the image of *Duende* in Spanish lore in its recognition of a presence, where the experience of immanence brings in the irrational, the absurd, the instinctive, and fate as other. The intimation of madness, the absent but present mother, the body, death, the world on the other side of the broken levee that became flashpoints for discussions of race – all constituted for me the feeling of an absent presence that was as big as Hurricane Katrina, the storm that devastated New Orleans on August 23–25, 2005. On the other hand, perhaps Hurricane Katrina as the phantom in the movie was the representation of the cataclysm.

This is the theme of *Beasts of the Southern Wild*, whose central protagonist is a six-year-old girl named Hushpuppy who lives with her father, Wink. She has lost her mother and lives in a shack with her father situated in the remote Delta. Wink is preparing his young daughter for the end of the world. When the father falls mysteriously ill, nature falls ill with him. Temperatures rise, the ice caps melt, and fearsome prehistoric beasts called *aurochs* run loose (an extinct species of large wild cattle that inhabited Europe, Asia, and North Africa). The aurochs appear in the film during and shortly after the storm's rising waters threaten to engulf their community, sending Hushpuppy in search of her long-lost mother. The movie depicts (although Romanized) the harsh reality of poverty and places the innocent little Black girl as the actual and symbolic victim of the storm, which is, psychically, indistinguishable from the racism that is as present in the background as the poverty, the storm that the broke through the levee that allows the nightmare to come rushing into our imagination. There is no containment for making sense of what's happening. We, as audience, like Hushpuppy and Wink, cannot offer any holding for either their or our feelings.

What a shocked world saw exposed in New Orleans in 2005 wasn't simply a broken levee. It was a cleavage of race and class, at once familiar and startlingly new, laid bare in a setting where they suddenly amounted to matters of life and death.

In this chapter I introduce the concept of the *phantom* as an image related to collective dynamics that operate as largely background in our cultural life. These are preliminary thoughts as I introduce yet another concept into the discussion of cultural complexes. But I hope it is one that will deepen our understanding, reflections, and discussion on the activity and dynamics of the group at the level of cultural processes.

Contemporary culture is a Tower of Babel of competing assumptions and ideologies about human rights, individual and group tensions around differences, resources, and intergroup conflicts both within and between nations, genders, and religions. These tensions produce complex moral and ethical dilemmas and push us toward political conflicts and social splits that we use to include and exclude each other. But what are we to do with all this? How do we process these times? Think about this? What actions can we take?

The one thing that seems to be missing in our Tower of Babel is a psychological attitude that allows us to see and to relate to what the unconscious is doing with these cultural ferments. In other words, what is missing is a psychological attitude toward the psyche expressed at the cultural level.

We tend to acknowledge the psychology of scapegoat dynamics but then feel powerless to do much with this awareness. Hate, envy, paranoia, and our difficulty with understanding and working with differences bind us over and over again to old patterns of relating based in fear. Previously, I introduced the concept of the cultural complex with the hope of opening up larger areas for viewing and getting language for describing what the psyche is doing with the interplay of these cultural phenomena. Building on the work of Joseph Henderson on the cultural unconscious (1990) and C. G. Jung's work on complexes (1934/1969) and the archetypal unconscious, the cultural complex allow us first to understand better how the psyche operates at the group level to organized group phenomena. Second, it allows us to understand both the individual's relationship to the group as well as how the group functions within the individual. Third, through attention to group complexes, we may come into a better relationship with the autonomy of the psyche as it plays itself out at individual and cultural levels, expressed as collective myths, images, and themes.

Background of my interest in cultural phantoms

Before moving on to say what I mean by *phantoms*, I want to present some of the background that helped me to get into these ideas. My first recognition that the group psyche had a stake in individual and group survival occurred through a dream on the night before my admission's interview to the C. G. Jung Institute of San Francisco.

> In the dream, I was sitting in a mosque with a dozen or so African American men, all dressed in black suits. I recognized them as Black Muslims. My name was called, and I got up and approached the door to leave for my interview. Suddenly, these men jumped between me and the door and said they would not let me pass until I demonstrated to them the secret handshake, and they would know that I knew them and would not forget them.

When a dream stirs up and reverberates through many levels of the psyche, as this one did for me, one can be relatively sure that something of the numinous and the archetypal has been activated. This kind of dream puts us in the shoes of that archetypal situation where we may resonate with the deeper currents of the living reality of the psyche. This living reality for me included recognition that the group, the African American community, was making a claim on me. That claim is something that I have been responding to and living out for many years. I have come to feel that it was a call for a reconnection to my Black ancestors that would open me up to my greater identity that comes through experiencing the reality of the psyche at the level of the group where symbols are embodied in our ways of living our values, identity, and integrity.

This dream brought to my attention the historical setting in which my current choice was situated. It forced me to remember the cultural assaults on our Black American humanity – hence, the title of one of my first papers on cultural complexes: "The Myth of Invisibility." I thought of the earlier Black authors who had touched me and the titles of their works: W. E. B. Du Bois's *The Souls of Black Folks*, Ralph Ellison's classic novel *Invisible Man*, James Baldwin's *Nobody Knows My Name*,

Toni Morrison's *Beloved*, all sharing the horrific dilemmas that are created in coping with collective hate, and the list goes on and on. Surely the theme that constitutes these authors' responses to American cultural life is that of invisibility, rootlessness, and homelessness. So I move through cultural complexes to the *phantom* or, as Borges (1999) says, from nightmare to dream, that is, to the presence of something from the facts of collective traumas to a way of working psychologically with their reality. My dream brought to my consciousness the importance of holding a connection to these ancestors/brothers as I go forward. My dream reflected an inner identity and a continuity that must be attended to and its shadow of collective responsibility and guilt as I moved from one frame of identity toward integrating another.

I am reminded of President Obama's report of his first trip to Kenya, before he went to Harvard Law School. He sensed his father's ghostly presence in the streets of Nairobi: "The Old Man's here, I think, although he doesn't say anything to me. He's here asking me to understand" (Obama, 1995, p. 323). Later he said, "The pain I felt was my father's. My questions were my brothers' questions. Their struggle, my birthright" (p. 430). These kinds of internal responses to transitions around identity and culture must be very common, even if they are minimized. For what Cornel West says of Black culture is true of any people whose cry is for being seen:

> The original cry of the black culture is neither a word nor a book, not an architectural monument or legal brief. Instead, it is a guttural cry and a wrenching moan – a cry not so much for help as for home, a moan less out of complaint than for recognition.
>
> (West, 1999, p. 81)

This chapter is part of an ongoing response to this request to remember and to share with others as I have integrated these kinds of reflections into my development as an analyst over the past number of years.

History-keeping by the unconscious in individuals and groups seems independent of the conscious intention and goals of the group, and there seems to be a teleological aspect also (Stein, 1987). There is an independence from space/time coordinates reflecting a nonsequential, transpsychic arrangement of historical patterns as these are related to individual complexes. Like phantoms, history is a strange attractor (*strange attractors* are hidden islands of structure, subtle patterns of order at the heart of chaos).

Jung's idea of history includes not only childhood and the immediate family, but also the larger matrix of culture, generational patterns, and archaic history as embedded in the collective unconscious. Inclusion of archetypes within the historical nexus led me to the realization that the influence of history on individuals is ubiquitous, rooted in culture and the unconscious, and pervasive through all segments of emotional and mental functioning, and is therefore fundamental to identity.

My first approach to history began with considering intergenerational traumas that I ultimately felt to be organized around cultural complexes. Thinking in intergenerational terms raises the issue of how all this occurs: by what mechanisms does the transmission happen? Since we are talking generally about the movement from past to present, across time dimensions, how do we talk about the fact that without direct communication we may be affected by processes and dynamics from another time and place? In addition, what about the intersubjective? And how do our ways of relating to each other stimulate and generate associations and complex responses that put us into different emotional spaces and awaken memories of the Other as well as our relationship to others past and present? These kinds of questions come up routinely in the transference-countertransference clinical situation. At a deeper level this seems to be related to generational continuity and, of course, to the survival of a people, group, or religion. Henderson, who introduced the concept of the cultural unconscious, defined it as

> an area of historical memory that lies between the collective unconscious and the manifest pattern of the culture. It may include both these modalities, conscious and unconscious, but it has some kind of identity arising from the archetypes of the collective unconscious, which assists in the formation of myth and ritual and also promotes the process of development in individuals.
>
> (1990, p. 102)

The part of Dr. Henderson's definition of the cultural unconscious that I am drawn to has to do with "some kind of an identity arising from the archetypes, which assists in the formation of myth and ritual and promotes the process of development in individuals." The term *phantom* is my response to "what kind of identity arising from the archetypes" as expressed through the cultural unconscious. In the remainder of this chapter, I describe what the phantom means and how it relates to cultural complexes.

The background to my thinking about the phantom can be found in Jung's own work described in his doctoral dissertation, entitled "On the Psychology and Pathology of So-Called Occult Phenomena"

(1902/1970), which laid the foundation for some of his most important concepts: subpersonalities, that is, autonomous complexes; the representation of an unconscious perception in the formation of imagery and personification; the autonomous psyche; images and hallucinations as potentially healing; and the mythical. Today we are likely to describe words like *phantom* in terms of the exteriorizations of unconscious complexes. Nearly twenty years later he said, "I doubt whether an exclusively psychological approach can do justice to the phenomena in question" (Jung, 1920/1969, para. 600, fn. 15). Jung's work at that time occurred when Freud's concerns about the uncanny expressed his attempt to understand the origins of certain psychic phenomena. The tilt toward scientific, rational understanding of phenomena that straddled the fence between the rational and the unknown put many of the earlier intuitions into the background for Freud (1919/1959) and was to lead to Jung's professional marginalization in the larger psychoanalytic community. Both Jung and Freud were interested in the psychic background, mostly the transpsychic for Jung and the more personal unconscious for Freud. However, Avery Gordon (1997), nearly a century later in using Freud's paper "The Uncanny," posited: "The uncanny is the return, in psychoanalytic terms of what the concept of the unconscious represses: the reality of being haunted by worldly contacts" (p. 54). "Something has become unfamiliar to describe those singular yet repetitive instances when home becomes unfamiliar, when your bearings on the world lose direction, when the over-and-done-with comes alive, when what's been in your blind spot comes into view" (Gordon, 1997, p. xvi). The phantom is the unbearable, that which is too much for consciousness, the untranslatable, that felt presence of the absence that opens the space for phantom dynamics.

Phantoms

Just as within individual psychology we may think about the imago of a mother or father complex, in cultural complexes we may think in terms of phantoms as constellations of images representing the psyche at the level of the group, expressed through social attitudes and structures that are alive in current events. For instance, the history of cultural traumatic events that have destroyed and disrupted social and cultural patterns causing breakdowns in family and social functioning have created symptoms of cultural traumas that can be seen in the varieties of learned helplessness, passivity, and lack of efficacy in relationship to one's own environment or world. Expectations of failure, anger, and a shift toward

external locus of control, self-blame, poor self-esteem, and the generation of invisibility – these can be witnessed on the individual level.

All of this occurs within a cultural setting of political, economic, and
institutional power structure that privileges certain groups over others.
I like the term *social suffering* from medical anthropology, introduced
by Arthur Kleinman, Venna Das, and Margaret Lock. The term allows
me to visualize the structural situations that freeze cultural complexes:

> Social suffering results from what political, economic and insti-
> tutional power does to people and, reciprocally, from how these
> forms of power themselves influence responses to social problems.
> Included under the category of social suffering are conditions that
> are usually divided among separate fields, conditions that simulta-
> neously involve health, welfare, legal, moral and religious issues.
>
> (1997, p. ix)

Another way to translate this is that trauma is perpetuated not only by victims
but also by those who are heirs to the benefits and privileges of the spoils as
they perpetuate attitudes, rituals, and the social machinery that makes these
conditions manifest and recurrent. I call these *phantomatic effects*.

My first hypothesis is intergenerational processes are expressed as
phantoms that provide representation and continuity for unresolved or
unworked-through grief and violence that occurred in a prior historical
cultural context, providing for potential continuity of these dynamics.
There are several sources of influence for my interest in phantoms. I will
mention only four.

For a number of years I had been working to utilize the concept of
complexes to better understand psychologically a variety of historical,
political, and cultural situations as these manifested in therapy and analysis. These included transference and countertransference issues, and representations of nonwhite groups as well as the relative unconsciousness
of whiteness. From this, I eventually formulated the concept of cultural
complexes. Cultural complexes as opposed to individual complexes are
group based. Like individual complexes, they function autonomously
within each individual and group to organize the attitudes, emotions, and
behavior that make up group life. Their archetypal telos seems to be
to provide both individuals and groups with a sense of belonging and
identity within a historical continuity of shared emotional assumptions.
The first influence came from my study of the unconscious dimensions
of group life. Over the years I have both consulted to groups and trained
others to read the unconscious dynamics of groups. One can see fairly

easily what Bion called the interaction between the more conscious way in which group members function to work with the group tasks and the unconscious processes that get going when members generate phantasies that are designed to create manageable anxiety for themselves. Essentially one sees the vastness and boundlessness of group life.

The second influence on my thinking came from my early work in a child guidance clinic as a child and family therapist wherein I adopted a family systems approach to the issues presented by my child patients. I often worked with families and many times extended family members as well as previous generations, such as grandparents. There I saw how family myths and beliefs led to emotional entanglements that bound family members to the needs and losses of previous generations. It became second nature to adopt at least a three-generational point of view within any family meeting. There was the child, and there was the family history of the parents that became a part of the contextual understanding of the presenting problem.

Not only did symbols and images of family members tend to encode intergenerational processes, but in the family unconscious suffering was shared or carried for each other; roles and rules were enacted that protected familial homeostasis and safety, often through extruding and scapegoating other members. I could always find the hero and the villain, the princess and the dirty old man, within the family group. I came to think of this unconscious functioning in the family as one expression of the cultural unconscious. The cultural unconscious at the family level embodies the interactional energies and strategies occurring within the family constellation, expressed through shared images, experiences, and roles. Like the cultural unconscious, the family unconscious expresses a shared emotional field at the group level, expressed through collective assumptions. The family's emotional life is intermingled with the cultural unconscious and with cultural processes.

The third contribution to my understanding of phantoms grew out of developing a way to look at intergenerational processes through a Jungian frame. As a transpersonal psychology, Jung's psychology serves as a corrective to the reductionist approaches of traditional psychoanalysis, which would reduce all human misery and mystery to developmental processes occurring after birth. To quote Jung, "the human psyche is not a self-contained and a wholly individual phenomena, but also a collective one" (1966/1972, para. 235). We would get closer to the truth if we think of the conscious personal psyche as resting upon a broad psychic base of inherited and universal psychic dispositions, which are unconscious. A child is related not only to parents but to grandparents and great grandparents; this explains the individuality of children more than the relationship to their own parents. In spite of Jung's explicit statements that our individual psyches emerge out of the deeper levels of the unconscious and are derived from the collective, communal, and social experiences of humankind (meaning our individual identity is grounded in the symbols, rituals, language, and shared historical memories of our families, countries, and nations), we still tend to think in terms of oppositions: 1) inner and outer, 2) psyche and social, 3) and a tendency to understand the outer in terms of individual psychodynamics.

The fourth influence came when I later discovered the work of Nicolas Abraham and Maria Torok (two French analysts) who described a topographical structure called the "phantom":

> It is a structure that grows out of secrets concealed and held. These secrets are silently transmitted directly into the unconscious of the child. The phantom is thus a formation totally outside any strictly phased or developmental view of human behavior. The child haunted by a phantom becomes a living tomb, in which an unspeakable drama, experienced as traumatic by someone else, lies buried yet alive, exerting its disruptive influence. It is described as a preservative repression. Along with the transgenerational transmission of a secret, the child inherits the unspoken imperative to preserve intact the integrity of that secret. The carrier of a phantom in analysis is thus always, metapsychologically speaking, "a child in analysis." To put it another way, the analysis of a phantom is always a child analysis. At the same time however the psychoanalysis of a phantom is also always an adult analysis – not an analysis of the adult on the couch but of the adult who concealed the secret.
>
> (Abraham & Torok, 1994, p. 140)

Abraham and Torok's work focused on the phantom within the intrafamilial situation. I use and extend it to cultural and collective forces. In Toni Morrison's *Beloved*, the dead child functions as a phantom representing the dynamics of slavery and its historical legacy for the intersubjective family life while simultaneously representing the cultural complex created around the existence of slavery.

The phantom as an imago

The phantom as an imago "has a living independence in the psychic hierarchy, i.e., possesses that autonomy which wide experience has shown to be the essential feature of feeling-toned complexes" (Jung, 1934/1969, para. 44, fn. 4). Phantoms function like complexes through the power of the imagination, potentially linking individual and group into a cultural narrative as organized by cultural complexes. Archetypal core and personal experiences may be split in the carrier of the phantom. In this regard I relate to Jung's work on spirits and soul. Jung in "The Psychological Foundations of Belief in Spirits" compares the experiences of complexes with the primitive belief in souls and spirits. Souls correspond to the autonomous complexes of the personal unconscious, and spirits to those of the collective unconscious. He makes an important distinction between soul complexes and spirit complexes:

> Whilst spirits are felt to be strange and as not belonging to the ego, this is not true of the soul or souls. The primitive feels the proximity or the influence of a spirit as something uncanny or dangerous, and is greatly relieved when the spirit is banished. Conversely, he feels the loss of a soul as if it were a sickness; indeed, he often attributes serious physical diseases to loss of soul.
>
> (1920/1969, para. 586)

In short, soul complexes "belong to the ego and the loss of them appears pathological" (para. 587).

Bringing this distinction into a reflection again on Morrison's *Beloved* (1987), the interaction between soul and spirit at the level of cultural complexes generates phantoms. The ghost Beloved, the infant daughter who was killed by her mother, Sethe, to prevent her from becoming a slave, returns to haunt the house, the mother, and the sister, Denver. Morrison's story is based on Margaret Garner, who did kill her two-year-old daughter rather than see her become a slave. This process is a reflection of a kind of introjective identification by which a people can accept a foreign thing into their identity. It can also be seen as a kind of effect of a collective projective identification, where the disowned and devalued is put into the "Other." Beloved's presence leads to the deterioration of Sethe's resources and ultimately to a community intervention made up of ostracized Black women who come to pray for Sethe. Hence, intergenerational transmission is a partially structured process that not only has been internalized and perpetuated, but also is a reflection of a type of psychic structure. Like fish in water, all of this tends to function in the background as Bollas's "unthought known" (1987). However, it is represented as a present absence, that is, as a phantom. As a phantom, Beloved has an autonomy that is uncanny. The spirit side of the phantom is expressed through its archetypal autonomy; the soul side of the phantom reflects its interpersonal and familial history. Both aspects work together to generate a connection through the cultural complex to cultural and group issues that may give rise to consciousness related to belongingness, identity, continuity, and community. Obviously, all these areas and dynamics carry the shadow elements. They also tend to carry the two-sidedness of a positive side, that is, belonging and identity, along with the concerns with losing oneself and fears of exclusion. These polarities stimulate projection, aggression, and competition. But in either case, they carry the potential for individuation and transformation of social forces. A phantom expresses a link to the cultural unconscious. To become aware of a phantom is to find the dynamics of the cultural unconscious.

Like the movie *Beasts of the Southern Wild*, Hurricane Katrina came to symbolize more than a natural disaster. When we think back on the horrific images that appeared on our television screens of thousands of people huddled in the New Orleans Superdome for shelter, food, and safety, while others waited on rooftops to be rescued, we are struck that the preponderance of these images are of African Americans. What a shocked world saw exposed in New Orleans in 2005 wasn't just a broken levee. It was a cleavage of race and class, at once familiar and startlingly new, laid bare in a setting where they suddenly amounted to matters of life and death (Deparle, 2005).

Gallup polls following the hurricane showed that most Black people felt that race was a key factor in the perceived failure of the government to respond to their situation. What reality wants is that we discover that when we are looking at it, we are at the same time looking at us: humans mirror outside reality, and reality mirrors our soul. No separation, just correspondence. This idea is so ancient (Gambini, 2003). Katrina in its primal form, like the flood in *Beast of the Southern Wild*, is the expression of a phantomatic complex situation with many layers – both a phantom and a cultural complex. In this way of relating to psyche we are in a position to begin turning nightmares into dreams (Ogden, 2004).

References

Abraham, N., & Torok, M. (1994). *The shell and the kernel: Renewals of psycho-analysis*. Chicago, IL: University of Chicago Press.

Bollas, C. (1987). *The shadow of the object*. New York, NY: Columbia University Press.

Borges, J. L. (1999). *Selected poems*. Harmondsworth: Viking Press.

Deparle, J. (2005, September 4). What happens to a race deferred. *The New York Times*. Retrieved from www.nytimes.com/

Freud, S. (1919/1959). *Standard edition, Collected papers: Vol. IV. The uncanny.* New York, NY: Basic Books.

Gambini, R. (2003). *Soul and culture.* College Station, TX: Texas A&M University Press.

Gordon, A. (1997). *Ghostly matters: Haunting and the sociological imagination.* Minneapolis, MN: University of Minnesota Press.

Henderson, J. (1990). The cultural unconscious. In *Shadow and self: Selected papers in analytical psychology.* Asheville, NC: Chiron.

Jung, C. G. (1902/1970). On the psychology and pathology of so-called occult phenomena. In W. McGuire (Ed.), *The collected works of C.G. Jung: Vol. 1. Psychiatric studies.* Princeton, NJ: Princeton University Press.

Jung, C. G. (1920/1969). The psychological foundations of belief in spirits. In W. McGuire (Ed.), *The collected works of C.G. Jung: Vol. 8. The structure and dynamics of the psyche.* Princeton, NJ: Princeton University Press.

Jung, C. G. (1934/1969). A review of the complex theory. In W. McGuire (Ed.), *The collected works of C.G. Jung: Vol. 8. The structure and dynamics of the psyche.* Princeton, NJ: Princeton University Press.

Jung, C. G. (1966/1972). Phenomena resulting from the assimilation of the unconscious. In W. McGuire (Ed.), *The collected works of C.G. Jung: Vol. 7. Two essays on analytical psychology.* Princeton, NJ: Princeton University Press.

Kleinman, A., Das, V., & Lock, M. (Eds.). (1997). *Social suffering.* Berkeley, CA: University of California Press.

Morrison, T. (1987). *Beloved.* New York, NY: Alfred A. Knopf.

Obama, B. (1995). *Dreams from my father.* New York, NY: Times Books.

Ogden, T. (2004). This art of psychoanalysis. *International Journal of Psychoanalysis, 85*(4), 857–877.

Stein, M. (1987). Looking backward: Archetypes in reconstruction. In M. Stein (Ed.), *Archetypal processes in psychotherapy.* Willamette, IL: Chiron Publications.

West, C. (1999). Black strivings in a twilight civilization. In *The Cornel West reader* (pp. 87–118). New York, NY: Basic Civitas Books.

Zeitlin, B. (Director). (2012). *Beasts of the southern wild* [Motion picture]. United States: Fox Searchlight Picture.

Chapter 2

Floating worlds and their phantoms in the aftermath of social catastrophes

The Invisible Men, an Inuit poem by Nakasuk
There is a tribe of invisible men
Who move around us like shadows – have you felt them?
They have bodies like ours and live just like us,
Using the same kind of weapons and tools.
You can see their tracks in the snow sometimes
And even their igloos
But never the invisible men themselves.
They cannot be seen except when they die
For then they become visible.

In this chapter I use the well-known evocative image of the "floating world" as context to look at the kinds of psychic presences that though normally invisible make themselves known during and after catastrophic social and cultural situations. The floating world is another world that both parallels and interpenetrates our ordinary world. Its intimations are sensed and become visible through images, art, lifestyle, and poetry – particularly haiku. The presences I want to make visible are what I am calling *phantom narratives*, or archetypal story formations, which are expressions of lived experiences.

As examples illustrating the floating world and the appearance of presences, I draw on William Lloyd Parry's account in the *London Review of Books* (2014), "Ghosts of the Tsunami," his report on the natural catastrophe caused by the Fukushima tsunami and earthquake that occurred in March 2011, in Okuma, Fukushima, Japan. Although there are different estimates of the number of fatalities (somewhere between 22,000 and 29,000), we know there was widespread physical destruction and disruption of human life. In addition, I will share two dreams I had in 2015, one in response to my taking up the study of the Fukushima disaster and a second that arrived in the aftermath of the murders of nine African American church members in Charleston, South Carolina, during a church prayer service. As background, I want to use the words of the title of Kazuo Ishiguro's (1986) unforgettable novel, *An Artist of the Floating World*, to give form to the kind of attitude toward sociocultural processes that has shaped my subjectivity. His achievement allowed me to open to my own imagination the Fukushima catastrophe. I also make use of Haruki Murakami's book of short stories, *After the Quake* (2002), particularly his story "UFO in Kushiro." These Japanese artists have offered me a helpful context for looking at a variety of psychic presences and their phantom narratives that appear in the aftermath of natural and social catastrophes.

A brief history of the "floating world"

The "floating world" refers to a period of time in Japan's history (1603–1857) when the people of Edo (now called Tokyo) enjoyed peace, prosperity, and the space to develop a heightened interest in popular arts, nature, and pleasurable things. The social hierarchy of the day, officially established by shogun rulers, placed the merchants, who were the wealthiest segment of the population, at the lower end of the scale. Their political power removed, the merchant class turned to art and culture as arenas in which they could participate on an equal basis with the elite upper classes (warriors, farmers, and artisans). This was a time of reversal of societal hierarchy. For instance, it was the collaboration among the merchants, artists, publishers, and townspeople of Edo that gave ukiyo-e artistry its unique culturally organizing power. The term *ukiyo-e* has many levels of meaning and interpretation that connect it to the sorrowful nature of our world, founded as it is in impermanence. We hear its voice in the classical haiku of Basho, Buson, and Issa. The Japanese character used for ukiyo-e connects to the floating, frivolous melancholy that surrounds the transitory nature of existence as we meet it in the everyday world. Ukiyo-e artwork reflects these themes.

Ukiyo-e provided a means of attaining cultural status outside the sanctioned class realms of shogunate, temple, and court for many different cultural groups within Japan. Ukiyo-e called up a world in constant flux that reflected contemporary tastes and concerns in uncanny yet familiar ways.

The term *floating world*, though referring both to a period in Japan's history and to the art and lifestyle during that period, expresses an implicitly Buddhist attitude toward existence, pointing to a nature that is transitory, impermanent, ever changing. It attempts to summon a human attitude toward these everyday phenomena that reflects the suffering that necessarily attends impermanence.

The following rather rueful haiku by Otomo Tabito (665–731) captures the spirit of the floating world:

Since all that lives
Must die someday,
I shall enjoy myself as long
as I remain in this world.

In this chapter I want to cross-reference another image, a modernist interpretation of our present cultural/global moment, a conception that comes close to the notion of the floating world. The sociologist Zygmunt Bauman has called ours "liquid times." To paraphrase him alchemically: we are in *solutio*, a phase of modernity in which "social forms" (structures) are changing in a way that they "can no longer [keep] their shape for long. . . . Socially sanctioned structures are unlikely to be given enough time to solidify and serve as frames of reference for human actions and long term strategies" (Bauman, 2007, p. 1).

One can hear in Zygmunt's words an echo of the impermanence and the transitoriness voiced in the Edo period by ukiyo-e.

Parry's "Ghosts of the Tsunami"

My initial impulse to write this paper emerged after reading Richard Lloyd Parry's account of the aftermath of the 2011 Fukushima earthquake and tsunami. Published in the *London Review of Books* (2014), it is titled "Ghosts of the Tsunami." There is certainly a story to tell. As we now know, the earthquake and tsunami left over 20,000 dead, caused massive destruction, and created a nuclear disaster when the active nuclear reactors shut down their sustained fission reactors. The emergency generators' cooling reactors overheated and caused the release of radioactive material. The Fukushima Nuclear Accident Independent Investigation Commission (NAIIC) found that the causes of the accident had been foreseeable and that the plant operator, Tokyo Electric Power Company (TEPCO), had failed to meet basic safety requirements such as risk assessment, preparing for containing collateral damage, and developing evacuation plans. Those are the material facts.

Parry's account focuses on the spiritual story. The reported appearances of ghosts and many instances of spirit possession among survivors affected large numbers of Japanese people in the time following the tsunami and earthquake. Most of the stories he reports were shared with him by Reverend Kaneda, a Buddhist priest, who acted consciously as a shaman to free the trapped Japanese spirit and to help individuals find whatever peace they sought. In addition to individual meetings with survivors, Reverend Kaneda tried meetings as a community group. This humane effort was at first greeted with silence, but then . . .

> Haltingly, apologetically, then with increasing fluency, the survivors spoke of the terror of the wave, the pain of bereavement and their fears for the future. They also talked about encounters with the supernatural. They described sightings of ghostly strangers, friends and neighbors, and dead loved ones. They reported hauntings at home, at work, in offices and public places, on the beaches and in the ruined towns. The experiences ranged from eerie dreams and feelings of vague unease to cases . . . of outright possession.

Parry notes:

> When opinion polls put the question, "How religious are you?" the Japanese rank among the most ungodly people in the world. It took a catastrophe for me to understand how misleading this self-assessment is. It is true that the organized religions, Buddhism and Shinto, have little influence on private or national life. But over the centuries both have been pressed into the service of the true faith of Japan: the cult of the ancestors.

Parry reflects on the fact that though the Japanese are able to think of themselves as the least religious people in the world, they have altars to their ancestors in their homes, which he had always assumed were mere decoration. These altars, after the catastrophe, became places where the ancestors were invited in, offered food and incense. Parry's conclusion is that the dead are not as dead in Japan as they tend to be in in Western societies. He laments with his subjects:

> The tsunami did appalling violence to the religion of the ancestors. Along with walls, roofs and people, the water carried away household altars, memorial tablets and family photographs. Cemetery vaults were ripped open and the bones of the dead scattered. Temples were destroyed, along with memorial books listing the names of ancestors.

And he adds:

> When people die violently or prematurely, in anger or anguish, they are at risk of becoming gaki, "hungry ghosts," who wander between worlds, propagating curses and mischief. There are rituals for placating unhappy spirits, but in the aftermath of the disaster few families were in a position to perform them. And then there were those ancestors whose descendants were entirely wiped out by the wave. Their comfort in the afterlife depended entirely on the reverence of living families, which had been permanently and irrevocably cut off: their situation was as helpless as that of an infant.

Thus, the Fukushima disaster created its own floating world in which ancestors and ghosts appeared. I was particularly interested in the ambiguity and sometimes conflation of the two terms *ghosts* and *ancestors* in Parry's article. In exploring the relationship between ghosts and ancestors, I began to wonder if this was more than a simple conflation of the terms and reflected the operation of a kind of cultural complex (Singer & Kimbles, 2004). That is, is Parry speaking about both ghosts and ancestors as the same, or does he mean they were different presences? It is this question I want to explore by way of using it as an example of what I have come to regard with resonating conceptual fluidity as *phantom narratives, floating worlds*, and *phantomatic spirit possessions*.

Some of these terms have emerged out of what I have witnessed within psychotherapy groups and analytic training groups and in a variety of consultations to organizations. I originally explained the phenomena I observed that seemed to belong to another narrative as expressions of cultural complexes. Such complexes give energy to what Joseph Henderson called the *cultural unconscious*. Following up on Henderson's formulation of the cultural unconscious in the light of Jung's complex theory helped me to think about and work with the expressions and manifestations of the unconscious at the level of the group as the manifestation of cultural complexes. Grounded in historical memory, the cultural unconscious, structured through cultural complexes, provided to my mind a kind of living continuity between past and present. This continuity is, as Murray Stein says, "the story of meaning, in which time and eternity, consciousness and unconsciousness, specific historical processes form a kind of living formation of images, histories in which individuals and cultural processes overlap" (Stein, 1987, p. 71). Such formations I later termed "phantom narratives" (Kimbles, 2014).

Murray Stein states that "Traditional persons live wholly inside such a sacred history; modern persons live wholly outside; postmodern persons, such as Jung was, dwell both inside and outside, carrying the tension of the opposing perspectives in a single paradoxical vision" (1987, p. 70). That formulation seems to express precisely aspects of the historical attitude I have been employing to explore phantom narratives. I see phantom narratives as activated processes of history that create symbolic spaces in which cultural memories and events are held in the lives of individuals, are elaborated, and come to signify the spirit of an entire interdependent group. Phantom narratives are modes of remembering and recognizing the group spirit that is more or less conscious when enacted as rituals of commemoration, ceremonies, and national anniversaries. Celebrating everything from the founding of the country, to victories of war, to the naming of streets and libraries after heroes, can evoke these narratives, which then become living monuments to a history that represents the group. On the other hand, within the same narratives there are modes of remembering that are more or less unconscious but form part of the connective tissue that binds the group and individuals together. Both conscious and unconscious aspects of such narratives form an interconnected worldview composed of shared history, values, rules, outlook, and sense of group spirit within an affective field organized around phantasies of inclusion/exclusion, victimization/dominance, and scapegoating. This living tissue becomes a zeitgeist – the spirit of a particular historical time and place capable of haunting the future. Phantom narratives become background processes that provide orienting images for our ideologies, beliefs, and affective valences toward particular leaders and the like. They link personal and social aspects of unconscious story, the memory that links the individual to the otherwise forgotten history of his or her social group. To quote Jung:

> When we look at human history, we see only what happens on the surface, and even this is distorted in the faded mirror of tradition. But what has really been happening eludes the enquiring eye of the historian, for the true historical event lies deeply buried, experienced by all and observed by none. It is the most private and most subjective of psychic experiences. Wars, dynasties, social upheavals, conquests, and religions are but the superficial symptoms of a secret psychic attitude unknown even to the individual himself, and transmitted by no historian.
>
> (Jung, 1934/1964, para. 315)

Phantom narratives are not archetypes, but rather expressions of the personal unconscious responding to the cultural unconscious, showing psyche's way of narrating the individual's relationship to his or her most essential social group. The phantom narrative provides an uncanny sense of community through its expression of enduring social and political issues, even when a community has consciously moved on from caring about them. I believe the psychic presences that appeared to so many people in the aftermath of the Fukushima earthquake and tsunami were such phantoms. The narratives they brought with them opened up an imaginative space for contemporary Japanese to reflect on the changes that have led to their current historical situation. They offered counsel with regard to the continuing problem of adaptation to an ocean-surrounded, earthquake-prone environment that has always shadowed the urbanization of Japanese culture. Avery Gordon, a sociologist of the imagination, comes close to my sense of the potential value of a phantom narrative when she says: "The ghost is not simply a dead or missing person, but a social figure, and investigating it can lead to that dense site where history and subjectivity make social life" (2008, p. 8). I will give some specific examples of this in the Japanese context.

Parry found on his return to the area where the tsunami had occurred evidence of both ghosts and disregarded ancestors. Both belonged to the symbolic and mythic world of embodied presences. Unlike internal objects, which have long been defined in psychoanalytic theory as internalized reflections of introjective and projective processes, ghosts and ancestors are external objects, the living dead that mirror our experiences of ourselves in our cultures, but remain stubbornly external to ourselves in our experience of them, as if they belong not to the self but to the world (Maiello, 2008). Thus, the altars that Parry realized were being used again in Japanese homes could be regarded as conduits to the intentions of the ancestors who had returned, places where families could relate to these Others not just through memory but in the present, beyond the usual constraints of death and time. To quote a line from Winnicott that has too often been ignored: "The ancestral heritage mediated through culture and stirred by the Zeitgeist provides continuity that transcends our personal existence" (1971, pp. 133–134).

In some coastal towns in Japan there stand stone tablets, which are from decades to centuries old, warning inhabitants not to build beyond a certain location. The stones stand as warnings about tsunamis that have struck here. Obviously previous inhabitants of this area experienced tsunamis and earthquakes. But the warnings these ancestors left future generations on their stone tablets seem to have gone unheeded. Parry reports the opinion, prior to the most recent tsunamis, that modern concrete constructions of stronger-than-ever stone walls on ocean shores could be trusted to prevent any lasting damage from a tsunami and even could withstand an earthquake. This, as we know, was not the case during the earthquake in Fukushima, where nuclear power plants were built in spite of the ancient warnings.

The writer Haruki Murakami, noting the failure on the part of some present-day policy makers in Japan to confront their arrogance in this regard, made a blunt association when he said in an interview in 2011 that Japan had "shirked its responsibility for its World War II aggression and the Fukushima nuclear disaster." Such a judgment sounds harsh to me, given a war in which there was also much aggression directed at Japan. In my view Murakami was raising his voice because he felt his country did not seriously pursue those who were really responsible for the 2011 crisis at Fukushima. He apparently felt the Fukushima plant was "the second major nuclear detriment that the Japanese people have experienced. . . . However, this time it was not a bomb being dropped upon us, but a mistake committed by our very own hands." This is harsh, but his voice enacts the role of a phantom in issuing a warning based on history. In a piece that appeared online in *The Guardian* titled "Murakami Laments Japan's Nuclear Policy" (Murakami, 2011), the novelist connects human action and inaction in not properly anticipating natural disaster to his country's failure to remember the devastation caused by the atomic bombings of Nagasaki and Hiroshima. He deliberately, as part of his polemic, summons a phantom narrative, the unacknowledged portion of national guilt for World War II, as his way to sound a warning. He wants to haunt his readers with the possibility that a similar fate of unacknowledged guilt may await those who ignore their responsibility for the risks attendant on nuclear energy. The novelist cannot find another way to express his anxiety as to what present abuses are being perpetuated in the name of peaceful energy than to compare intransigent nuclear energy policy to the war policy that invited a not fully anticipated nuclear attack by another power's war machine. Note how the phantom narrative has led a Japanese man to scapegoat his own country for its victimhood at the hands of a type of nuclear attack that it did not itself initiate.

We might feel better about Murakami's rhetoric by putting it into a broader psychological context that may make clearer what he is really worried about. A number of years ago Robert Jay Lifton spoke of how the appearance of "nuclear weapons in the mid-1940s evoke an image: that of man's extermination of himself as a species with his own technology"

(1987, p. 43). This extermination, he feels, must be distinguished from the "religious imagery of 'Armageddon,' 'Final Judgement' or 'the end of the world,'" for in those accounts humans are acted upon by a higher power. The shift that Lifton speaks to is the "danger that comes from our own hands" (p. 43). Widespread guilt, numbing, and doubts about our human connectedness are a consequence of self-destructive actions:

> For in a post-nuclear world, one can hardly be certain of living on in one's children or their children; in one's creations or human influences in some form of lasting spirituality . . . or in eternal nature, which we know to be susceptible to our weapons and pollutions.
>
> (p. 44)

To generalize from Murakami's words about the Japanese to Lifton's concerns about the influence of nuclear madness on all our planet's citizens, I turn to Jung's attempts to describe how a type of contagion occurs when evil is exposed. In an earlier statement reflecting on World War II Germany he said:

> The sight of evil kindles evil in the soul – there is no getting away from this fact. The victim is not the only sufferer; everybody in the vicinity of the crime, including the murderer, suffers with him. Something of the abysmal darkness of the world has broken in on us, poisoning the very air we breathe and befouling the pure water with the stale, nauseating taste of blood. True, we are innocent, we are the victims, robbed, betrayed, outraged; and yet for all that, or precisely because of it, the flame of evil glowers in our moral indignation.
>
> (Jung, 1945/1964, para. 410)

This is the psychology of mutual scapegoating. Jung and Lifton are commenting on the contagion involved in social suffering – that is, the generalized impact on the social network of the meaning of, and reaction to, the reality of this destructive potential. The radiation and nuclear disaster at Fukushima evoked again the present absent awareness of the overwhelming danger everyone on earth lives with every day. It is not just a Japanese problem.

This brings me back to Parry's use of ancestors and ghosts as interchangeable. The problem with that blurring of the distinction is that we may miss an opportunity to think about how we relate to and listen to the voices of our ancestors – or not. When do we listen? How do we engage their messages? How does awareness influence how we think about the relationship between our ancestors/ghosts and us? How do we hold the tension between our originality and their influence? Our indebtedness to them and our wish to be freed of their influence? This is indeed a dilemma. But, to quote Gordon, these are "ghostly matters" that haunt us at every turn. "To be haunted is to be tied to historical and social effects" (Gordon, 2008, p. 190).

In his paper on the seminal Freudian analyst Hans Loewald, Thomas Ogden underscores his psychoanalytic ancestor's idea of "parricide to refer to the act committed by one who murders a person to whom he stands in a specifically sacred relation, as a father, mother, or other near relative, or (in a wider sense) a ruler" (Ogden, 2009, p. 119). He uses the family setup to get at the presence of authority and how we relate to it. "It is a parental authority that is murdered; by that, whatever is sacred about the bond between child and parent is violated" (p. 129). "It is a faceoff between the generations, a life and death battle for autonomy, authority, and responsibility" (p. 121). Thus, the engagement between the generations takes place in the very process of coming to terms with the urge to grow or individuate. So, there is something at stake in looking at how we engage our ancestors. Is it ignoring them that turns them into ghosts that haunt us, causing us to blame ourselves for both past and present failures to get things right? This theme has been explored by others, including Madeleine Scherer, who writes about such phenomena in the wake of the Irish Independence movement, in which many murders had been committed:

> More terrifying than the return of ghosts may be the prospect that there is nothing to return, no survival, no resurrection, and no commanding voice from beyond the grave; as Žižek puts it, "it is not sufficient to say that we fear the spectre – the spectre itself already emerges out of a fear, out of our escape from something even more horrifying: freedom."
>
> (Žižek, 1994b, p. 27; cited in Scherer, 2015, p. 129)

Obviously, looking at the relationship between the generations in the Oedipal context favored by psychoanalysts, exploring a patient's personal past could easily apply to the intergenerational conflict between the living and the living dead in countries, and in us when our countries are at war with each other. Talking with Sonu Shamdasani about Jung's *Red Book*, written as World War I was becoming a reality, James Hillman says: "Opening the *Red Book* seems to be opening the mouth of the dead"; and Shamdasani answers Hillman: "He (Jung) comes to the realization that unless we come to terms with the dead we simply cannot live, and that our life is dependent on finding answers to their unanswered questions" (Hillman & Shamdasani, 2013, p. 1).

Listening to and dealing with the unanswered questions of the ancestors as we face present threats to our lives, not dissimilar from those they had to face, reflects continuity and an affirmation of life. Does denying and not listening to ancestors turn them into angry ghosts?

Obviously, Murakami knows this. Rosbrow says of Murakami's stories that they "frequently involve themes around loss, searching for the lost person, and haunting feelings of regret and awareness of transience" (2012, p. 215). In his book *After the Quake*, Murakami (2002) describes the effect on a number of characters of the 1995 Kobe earthquake that killed 5,000 people, changing millions of lives. A woman in his short story, "UFO in Kushiro," is trying to hold herself together in the aftermath of this event; each morning she gets up and stands vacantly in front of the television, looking at the destruction over and over again. Then she leaves her husband, explaining to him in a note that living with him was like living with a chunk of air and he was a box of empty air. Reading the story, I got the feeling that Murakami was describing two people who had become the living dead. He was dramatizing spirit possession. Life seems to have been taken out of both the woman and her husband. A phantom narrative has replaced their agency.

Murakami seems to be talking about something like this when he describes the importance of narratives for him as a writer:

> Now a narrative is a story, not logic, not science, nor philosophy. It is a dream you keep having, whether you realize it or not. Just as surely as you breathe, you go on ceaselessly dreaming your story. And in these stories you wear two faces. You are simultaneously subject and object. You are the whole and you are a part. You are real and you are shadow. "Storyteller" and at the same time "character." It is through such multi-layering of roles in our stories that we heal the loneliness of being an isolated individual in the world.
>
> (Murakami, 2001, p. 231)

I hope you can see by the associations that I have pursued in examining the aftermath of the Fukushima tsunami how much a culture's perception of itself begins to take shape around what I have called a *phantom narrative*. I hope you also hear that such possession by the spirit of a past guilt or sorrow can only be undone by developing an authentic sense of the history involved. We hear the call to conscience in the phantom narrative right when we accept its call to review and reconsider our history, and we must try to do so in a human way, which we can start to do when we remember that our ancestors were once living humans too.

Two dreams

To make more personal the idea of this kind of integration of phantom narratives, I will share two dreams of my own. I had the first dream about a month before I began to write on the topic of this chapter:

> *I was in my analytic office (my first office in this particular building; I have since moved to another office roughly directly above my old office). As the dream opens many of my past and current patients as well as former and current colleagues are rushing into my office, having heard that a large tsunami would be striking Santa Rosa and they were taking back the things they had left with me. I was surprised at the desperate nature of those patients and colleagues and disoriented about the tsunami.*

This dream forces me to look at the effects of anticipated and actual disasters. The panic and fear expressed by those with whom our relationships had been a container and holding space for self and hope had been retroactively snatched back from the relationship, and I suspect to a place where there was no access to a holding environment. This is not a return to memory but to loss, to the "no one being there place." What kind of being or life is possible in a devastated, catastrophic time and place? It is a time of breakdown in the environmental holding, a madness that cannot be experienced. Psychotic greed. Again, to quote Winnicott:

> In using the word "culture" I am thinking of the inherited tradition. I am thinking of something that is in the common pool of humanity, into which individuals and groups of people may contribute, and from which we may all draw if we have somewhere to put what we find. . . . The interplay between originality and the acceptance of tradition . . . seems to be just one more example, and a very exciting one, of the interplay between separateness and union. The ancestral heritage mediated through culture and stirred by the Zeitgeist provides continuity that transcends our personal existence.
>
> (Winnicott, 1971, pp. 133–134)

Culture, then, is the ultimate container for conscious and unconscious reflection, and this makes sense, because it is the holding environment we cannot escape. By having this dream, which opens up a space of transcultural empathy, I have found myself able to hold recent Japanese history and to place it in a context of the world's, not just Japan's, unconsciousness. We share the shadow of disregarding our ancestors' warning about the danger greed has always posed to human settlement everywhere on the earth.

I will share with you a second dream that allows us to think about the issues of the catastrophe and phantoms in another kind of socially created devastated space. I had this dream following the murder of nine African American worshippers during a prayer meeting in Charleston, South Carolina, in 2015:

> *In this dream I approach a house with a screen-covered front porch. On the front porch, in the space between the outside and inside of the house, there is a figure there that reminds me of the killer of the nine church people. I am uncertain whether to call out to him to see if I could help him with something or if I should call the police, as his state of mind is unstable.*

During my preteen years, I lived in an African American community in the American South. There the front porch was a regular part of the design of many homes and the screen-enclosed space added a familiar intimacy to being outside and, strangely enough, inside simultaneously. It was a Winnicottian transitional space between inner private and public spaces, a space for hospitality and a light barrier, an enclosed space. People would sit and talk with other family members, nod to strangers, meet with friends and tell stories about ordinary daily events while sharing simultaneously judgments, attitudes, and prejudices. One could mark out a private space within a public world. What is inside and outside overlap in this private but social space.

This is the space my psyche created to place the young white man who murdered the nine Black church members during their prayer service. This kind of space, according to Winnicott, is indispensable for the development of psychic life in the maternal/infant relationship. It makes the cathexis of the outer world possible and the relationship to the inner world becomes affirmable as "who I am; who we are."

If we listen to Winnicott, our analytic ancestor, we have to realize that the inevitable frustrations of relating to the outer world can lead anyone to anger and aggression, and that the resultant destructiveness plays a role in the construction of much subsequent reality by putting the world as an object outside the self. Thus, aggression creates its own connection with the outer world, making of it an external object, and often one that one feels fully justified in scapegoating. In this breakdown of the world as the holding environment for psyche, however, the projected self survives as a phantom with uncanny power to speak to the self left behind. The phantom bears witness to the kinds of encapsulations, fragmentations, rages, and guilts that create the intolerable anxieties of a self no longer holding and held by the spirit of its ancestors, who were the holding environment of culture itself.

In my dream the young man who is its protagonist is caught in a no man's land, an unfamiliar space, that is, transitional space as potential space. There is no space for connecting or discovering the self in relationship. He has, to my mind, become a phantom. And yet the phantomatic complex that possesses him connects him and us to the larger cultural complexes around race and reveals that the issues around race relations have been full of lost unfound humans. I think of Richard Wright's *Native Son* (1940); James Baldwin's *Nobody Knows My Name* (1961); Ralph Ellison's *The Invisible Man* (1953); and the figure of Beloved, whom Sela called her "best thing," in Toni Morrison's book of the same name (1987). The phantom is the space we make for the disenfranchised, the stranger who feels alone. Then the outer collective of a culture offers no transitional space for the expression of creative agency, but instead an inexorable, engulfing dragon of demonic psychic processes, a maelstrom that catches our spirits and paralyzes our souls. Moving back and forth between passive, engulfed submission to consuming paranoid anxieties and fears is miserable, but it is the way so many now live their psychological lives in a world that no longer feels like a container and has often become a jail. In individuals, the rupture of their relationships to themselves reflects the rupture of their emotional continuity with the world. Often enough, they stalk the community, if only online, like phantoms, and ponder what aggressive revenge they might be able to enact.

We in America have long lived with the ongoing reality of a history of slavery that has not been emotionally worked with and engaged. This history continues to haunt our country. Thus, our modern floating world has seemed for too long, to use an image from Cornel West, to be like a serpent coiled around the legs of our national freedom that perpetuates a kind of ongoing haunting that barely moves, much less floats.

Following the Fukushima tsunami, Reverend Kaneda would chant the Buddhist Heart Sutra to all those who came in for solace and sought to be freed from their grief, expressed by some as possession by the spirits of strangers who were using the psyches of others to get a message back

home or to be freed. He would then finish with "come toward the light."
Here is the first part of the Heart Sutra:

> There are no eyes, no ears, no nose, no tongue,
> no body, mind; no colour, sound, or smell;
> no taste, no touch, no thing; no realm of sight,
> no realm of thoughts; no ignorance, no end to ignorance;
> no old age and no death;
> no end to age and death; no suffering,
> nor any cause of suffering, nor end.
> to suffering, no path, no wisdom and no fulfillment.

The following is one of many stories Parry reports (2014):

> "Kaori!" said the voice. "Kaori! I have to get to Kaori. Where are
> you, Kaori? I have to get to the school, there's a tsunami coming."
> The man's daughter had been at her school by the sea when the
> earthquake struck. He had rushed out of work and driven along the
> coast road to pick her up, when the water had overtaken him. His
> agitation was intense; he was impatient and suspicious of Kaneda.
> The voice asked: "Am I alive or not?"
> "No," Kaneda said. "You are dead."
> "And how many people died?" the voice asked.
> "Twenty thousand people died."
> "Twenty thousand? So many?"
> Later, Kaneda asked him where he was.
> "I'm at the bottom of the sea. It is very cold."
> "Come up from the sea to the world of light," Kaneda said.
> "But the light is so small," the man replied. "There are bodies all
> around me, and I can't reach it. And who are you anyway? Who are
> you to lead me to the world of light?"

I have no solution to the problem I have raised here, but I will close with
another Buddhist song different from the Heart Sutra but with a similar
sentiment:

> *Obon: Feeding the Hungry Spirits (Gates of Sweet Nectar),*
> *by Krishna Das*
>
> Calling out to hungry hearts.
> Everywhere through endless time
> You who wander, you who thirst

I offer you this Bodhi mind
Calling out to hungry spirits
Calling out to hungry hearts
All the lost and the left behind
Gather around and share this meal
Your joy and sorrow I make it mine.
It is the heart opening to all the lost and the left behind.

References

Bauman, Z. (2007). *Liquid times: Living in an age of uncertainty*. Cambridge: Polity Press.

Gordon, A. (2008). *Ghostly matters*. Minneapolis, MN: University of Minnesota Press.

Hillman, J., & Shamdasani, S. (2013). *Lament of the dead: Psychology after Jung's Red Book*. New York, NY: W.W. Norton.

Ishiguro, K. (1986). *An artist of the floating world*. London: Faber & Faber.

Jung, C. G. (1934/1964). The meaning of psychology for modern man. In *The collected works of C.G. Jung: Vol. 10. Civilization in transition*. Princeton, NJ: Princeton University Press.

Jung, C. G. (1945/1964). After the catastrophe. In *The collected works of C.G. Jung: Vol. 10. Civilization in transition*. Princeton, NJ: Princeton University Press.

Kimbles, S. (2014). *Phantom narratives: The unseen contributions of culture to psyche*. New York, NY: Rowman & Littlefield.

Lifton, R. J. (1987). The image of the end of the world: A psychohistorical view. In V. Andrews, R. Bosnak, & K. W. Goodwin, (Eds.), *Facing apocalypse*, Dallas, TX: Spring Publications.

Maiello, S. (2008). Encounter with a traditional healer: Western and African therapeutic approaches in dialogue. *Journal of Analytical Psychology, 53*(2), 241–260.

Murakami, H. (2001). *Underground: The Tokyo gas attack and the Japanese psyche*. New York, NY: Vintage Books.

Murakami, H. (2002). *After the quake*. New York, NY: Vintage Books.

Murakami, H. (2011, June 13). Murakami laments Japan's nuclear policy. *The Guardian*. Retrieved from htttps://www.theguardian.com/books/2011/jun/13/Murakami-japan-nuclear-policy

Ogden, T. H. (2009). Reading Loewald: Oedipus reconceived. In *Rediscovering psychoanalysis*. New York, NY: Routledge,

Parry, R. L. (2014, February 6). Ghosts of the tsunami. *London Review of Books, 36*(3), 13–17. Retrieved from www.lrb.co.uk/v36/n03/richard-lloydparry/ghosts-of-the-Tsunami

Rosbrow, T. (2012). Murakami's *After the quake* – The writer as waking dreamer and trauma analyst. *Psychoanalytic Dialogues, 22*, 215–227.

Scherer, M. (2015, December). All these presences: Haunting memory in post-Independence Irish poetry. *The Apollonian*, *2*(3). Retrieved from http://theapollonian.in/wp-content/uploads/2015/09/2.3.13.pdf

Singer, T., & Kimbles, S. (2004). *The cultural complex: Contemporary Jungian perspectives on psyche and society*. New York, NY: Routledge.

Stein, M. (1987). Looking backward: Archetypes in reconstruction. In N. Schwarz-Salant & M. Stein (Eds.), *Archetypal processes in psychotherapy* (pp. 51–74). Willamette, IL: Chiron Publications.

Winnicott, D. (1971). *Playing and reality*. London: Tavistock.

Chapter 3

Phantoms at the cultural level

Phantoms at the cultural level are imagoes that represent intergenerational forces. They offer us a way to understand the psychic processes concerned with history and time through providing continuity related to kinship libido (race, ethnicity, religion). Such kinship libido mediates the need to belong and have an identity within the human family system or a group organized by cultural complexes. Until engaged and made conscious through locating it within its lived context, kinship libido tends to function as a homelessness complex. Cultural complexes expressed through historical complexes not only create containers for phantoms but also have phantoms as their imagoes. Phantoms represent the archetypal spirit of the group (Singer, 2003). The emergence of phantoms is related to

> spirits of nature, but not the psychic factors that correspond to them, such as suggestibility, lack of criticism, fearfulness, propensity to superstition and prejudice – in short, all those qualities which make possession possible. Even though nature is depsychized, the psychic conditions which breed demons are as actively at work as ever. The demons have not really disappeared but have merely taken on another form: they have become unconscious psychic forces.
>
> (Jung, 1945/1964, para. 431)

I take this complicated set of thoughts from Jung to describe a type of dynamism operating at the level of the collective, generating processes (attitudes, prejudices, discrimination, and so on) that need to be encountered, taken on, and worked with. Phantoms are capable of possessing a group and the individual. Jung's description of the god Wotan (a Northern European mythological figure), in his *Essays on Contemporary Events* (1989), is his way of describing the collective madness that occurred in Nazi Germany. From my point of view, his description is a concretization of both an archetypal and cultural phantom at the heart of a cultural complex during the time of National Socialism.

In this chapter, I draw on Jung's statement to show that

- Generational issues are enfolded in complexes that function over time and outside a phased developmental view of human behavior. Though related to time, generational processes may be nonstratified, nonlinear, and irrational.
- The child is a mediator for ancestral processes.
- Generational processes are carried as psyche structures, not simply as memory traces.
- Absences, absent-presences, voids, and negative identities can all embody "psychic matter." They are entities from the third realm or group life as expressed through the cultural unconscious. Positively, this becomes transitional space (Winnicott), and negatively, a dead space as the past closes and dies.

Two example phantoms: *In Treatment*

In this section I use the term *phantom narratives* to describe an implicit narrative structured by cultural complexes

- That function more or less in the background, that is, mostly unconsciously through identifications, rituals, ideologies, and religious process.
- That can haunt the therapeutic process, group development and relationships, and cultural processes through creating a second dissociated narrative process that possesses the group.

In Treatment is an American HBO drama, produced by Rodrigo Garcia, about therapist Dr. Paul Weston and his weekly sessions with patients. I will use therapy sessions with one patient to point to the appearance of the phantom as an unconscious dynamic reflecting a cultural complex, both in the therapy and in the script itself. Though not stated as such, *In Treatment*'s second narrative thread (Garcia, 2008) of the African American pilot begins with a murder – a murder that took place in some other time and place, but the blood runs right through the interactions between the white therapist and the Black patient, Alex, and his father.

In the second episode, Alex shares with the therapist a story that his father told him. He describes an event in which his father, in an effort to protect the two of them from white vigilantes, "accidentally smothers him" – that is, he kills Alex's grandfather. The therapist does not address the cultural and/or historical aspect of the story. The narrative of this event only reappears when the father comes to see the therapist following his son's apparent suicide. He asks the therapist if his son told him about that particular situation. The father is full of guilt and is clearly haunted by the situation involving his own father. This is a complex, which he has transmitted to his son. And this is a particularly difficult situation for the therapist to work with, as the cultural complex aspect silently hovers in the background. The blood of the murdered father occurred both historically and again in his interaction with the therapist. At the level of the cultural and archetypal unconscious, it is the white patriarchy as dominance and privileged authority that kills. This phantom is in the room as part of the American cultural complex. The therapist does not acknowledge, much less address, the obvious cultural differences between himself and Alex or the significance of the difference in the story of his grandfather's death and his father's guilt over his role in his father's death when he was trying to protect them and his son's suicide, as all of this is framed within the unconscious dynamics of cultural racism. The therapist simply seems to be tone deaf. His lack of understanding keeps the second narrative unconscious, out of the conscious dialogue. Thus, the therapist colludes with the intergenerational murder of the healthy drive in Alex for understanding, emancipation, and the claiming of his own authority – the very situation that existed for the grandfather in the context of the Jim Crow culture at the time of his killing. This unacknowledged killing is what I call the *phantom aspect* of the cultural complex that haunts the therapy.

The father/son relationship embodies the generational issues around how authority is symbolized, who has it, how it is passed on, and the relationship to cultural roles and expectations. When this is perverted, the child gets little in the way of guidance and even less to appropriate as strength. In the case of Alex and his father/grandfather, there is the legacy of guilt between them, expressed on the part of the father about his contribution to his son's suicide – was he the killing father? Alex's father describes his son staring at him; his eyes reminded him of his own father. The containment in that relationship for the transmission of authority, autonomy, and responsibility was perverted by the background cultural complex activated around the unprocessed feelings related to the group trauma around race. The processing of this aspect would involve looking at guilt and complicity on the part of the therapist as a representative of the dominant social position. This is part of what haunts the initial disclosure about this event to the therapist and the father's disclosure to the therapist. The ghost is never identified and converted into an experience of actual loss and trauma.

Clinical situation: an overlapping phantomatic narrative

Recently, during a silent moment in my analytic work, a patient wondered out aloud:

> When a sound stops, at what point do the vibrations end in space? When does a terror experienced and shouted out end? Do the vibrations go on forever – resonating in others who get the story of what happened through some sort of intuitive feeling?

I asked him about the stimulus for these questions. He had in mind a past situation that we both knew about, in which a colleague had been killed during an outdoor sporting event. The patient had for several months been preoccupied with a vague anxiety about his own dying. But this way of expressing his anxiety was new and different. For one thing, it felt like a real question that opened both of us up to a kind of reverie about the unknown. This question was distinct from the anxious questions he had asked before, which had a stale circularity to them.

My patient's questions stimulated in me a set of thoughts and fantasies about the ongoing impact of trauma, individual and collective, and its intergenerational aftermaths. I, too, in a kind of half-conscious state, had been wondering how long traumas last and spread out in time. I realized that over the past several years, I had been pondering how group complexes get processed, mourned, and redeemed in groups and in individuals.

My patient had not yet been born when his parents fled Nazism in Germany before the Second World War, and he had never brought that aspect of his traumatic family history directly into his analysis, even though his family structured many of its activities around managing the parents' "irrational" expressions of anxiety through their participation in religious rituals. Something within his family remained unassimilated because the trauma they experienced when fleeing the Nazis in Germany was not acknowledged as an event that had a real psychic impact on their lives. A critical aspect of this patient's family history appeared to live on, encrypted, in his own generalized anxiety symptoms and in his anxiety about dying.

Through wondering aloud, was the patient asking himself/me about some family event that he knew about on some unconscious level but dared not let himself know consciously? Or was it the phantom of his family's secret and its repression that came into the session with his curiosity?

Winnicott indicated that catastrophes occur when there are disruptions to the infant's experience of continuity of its being. This creates a fissure in the infant's ontological status (Ogden, 2004). The kind of disruptions to which Winnicott calls our attention are *primitive agonies*, the unthinkable states of being that come about when these disruptions occur. Creating phantoms or images at the level of the cultural unconscious, the trauma disrupts the group's and individual's sense of going on being, of continuity. This disruption in continuity is surely one of the seeds that contributes to the dissociation of this second narrative.

Although quoted previously, it is worth quoting again; Jung says it in a slightly different way:

> The sight of evil kindles evil in the soul. . . . The victim is not the only sufferer; everybody in the vicinity of the crime, including the murderer, suffers with him. Something of the abysmal darkness of the world has broken in on us, poisoning the very air we breathe and befouling the pure water with the stale, nauseating taste of blood. . . . When evil breaks at any point into the order of things our whole circle of psychic protection is disrupted.
>
> (Jung, 1945/1964, para. 410)

Summary comments

Cultural complexes mediate the two-way relationship between cultural and social influences on the individual psyche as well as the individual's reciprocal impact on the culture. These complexes exist within the psyche of the collective as a whole and within the individual members of a group. On an individual level, cultural complexes are expressions of the need to belong and have a valued identity within the context of a specific reference group, even though this may lead to splitting, rigidities, and the whole range of phenomena that we recognize as psychological disturbances. At the level of the group, cultural complexes seem to offer cohesion, which provides a sense of kinship and group spirit. At the pathological extreme, this kinship is expressed in archetypal defenses of the group spirit.

In my work as an analyst and psychologist I have looked closely at how the activation of a cultural complex affects clinical narrative. The activation of a cultural complex means at least two related, interdependent things have become constellated: the individual and the group level of the psyche have become activated and structured by processes emanating from the collective unconscious functioning through cultural symbolic forms (beliefs, rituals, signs). I have long felt that these two activated poles (their bipolarity) generate the potential for a new form of intersubjectivity.

The group level of the psyche in the individual and the group level of the psyche of which the individual is in participation mystique or unconscious identity is a *dual unity*. The capacity to recognize the existence of a cultural complex depends on the recognition and appropriation of this space that has been created by this activation for the creation of a dialectic through which psychological consciousness can evolve. Neither the group level nor the individual level has a privileged position. This is a paradox at the heart of cultural human life.

There is a moral imperative at the heart of this work on developing consciousness of the role of cultural complexes, phantoms, and group dynamics. So much of our time sees the manifestation of differences as identity politics and ideological position. As terrible and concrete as all this seems, a core demand for most groups experiencing marginalization is for recognition of their worth and that of their culture. It is important to hear this as not only a material but also, more importantly, a psychological demand. From a Winnicottian point of view, what kind of facilitating, good-enough environment can we develop to hold and help facilitate the development of the type of consciousness that can work with phantoms and cultural complexes?

References

Garcia, R. (Writer and Director). (2008). Alex [Television series episodes]. In R. Garcia (Producer), *In Treatment*. New York, NY: HBO.

Jung, C. G. (1945/1964). After the catastrophe. In *The collected works of C.G. Jung: Vol. 10. Civilization in transition*. Princeton, NJ: Princeton University Press.

Jung, C. G. (1989). *Essays on contemporary events*. Princeton, NJ: Princeton University Press.

Ogden, T. H. (2004). The analytic third: Implications for psychoanalytic theory and technique. *Psychoanalytic Quarterly*, *73*(1), 167–195.

Singer, T. (2003). Cultural complexes and archetypal defences of the group spirit. In J. Beebe (Ed.), *Terror, violence, and the impulse to destroy* (pp. 191–209). Zurich: Daimon Verlag.

Chapter 4

Unbearable things, unseen

Viola Davis won Best Supporting Actress in 2017 for her role in the film *Fences*, adapted from August Wilson's play. Her acceptance speech sets the tone for this chapter:

> There's only one place where all the people are gathered with the greatest potential, that's the graveyard. People ask me all the time, what kind of stories you want to tell, Viola Davis? I say exhume those bodies, exhume those stories. Stories of the people who dreamed big and never saw their dreams to fruition; people who fell in love and lost. I became an artist, and thank god I did; we're the only profession who celebrate what it means to live a life. So here's to August Wilson who exhumed and exalted the ordinary people.

How do we respond to and deal with expressions of trauma and violence connected with racial suffering? These expressions grow out of the particular cultural and social realities that provide context for many of the symptoms and signs of individual suffering that we see frequently in our consulting rooms as well as in our society. For suffering is not simply a manifestation of private and personal pain. I use the concept of cultural complexes to help make visible the forces that operate implicitly in both our personal and cultural lives. These complexes also cross the areas of intergenerational processes and the role and function of collective shadow dynamics. These implicit structures, images, and forces are phantom narratives.

To understand the expressions of phantom narratives, we need to find a way to recognize the presence of the absence of emotional forces in our social and political lives. Toni Morrison expresses a kind of attitude toward these unconscious processes, called by Layton "normative" (Layton, 2008).

> We can agree, I think, that invisible things are not necessarily "not-there"; that a void may be empty, but it is not a vacuum. In addition, certain absences are so stressed, so ornate, so planned, they call attention to themselves; arrest us with intentionality and purpose, like neighborhoods that are defined by the population held away from them.
>
> (Morrison, 1989, p. 11)

I echo Viola Davis's statement to "tell our story." I began to tell aspects of my story, which became a way to tell our story in order to think about the activation of complexes in groups and cultural life that operate around differences: racial, ethnic, religious, gender, class, and privilege. The story I am telling is a psychological narrative that expresses themes about belonging, identity, identification, shadow, boundaries, otherness, and the striving for recognition.

In addition to this psychosocial narrative, I want to draw attention to a dimension that is full of moral connotations, such as good/bad and dirty/clean, and serves as a type of haunting super-ego around "shoulds," obligations, and injustices. Emotionally, the dynamics are structured by fear and fascination, possessiveness and disavowal, and shame and entitlement (or narcissism). We are acculturated by these cultural realities, and our cultural attitudes are absorbed long before we are conscious of them as factors in the structuring of our identities and subjectivities. Together these processes become "psychically charged and volatile" (Odajnyk, 1976, p. 36). Or in Jung's words: "Our fearsome gods have only changed their names: they now rhyme with -ism" (1969, para. 326). "For the true historical event lies deeply buried, experienced by all and observed by none. It is the most private and most subjective of psychic experiences (Jung, 1968, para. 315).

In a real way, cultural complex awareness and analysis allows us to explore the primal aspect of a network of tangled individual, group, and cultural/psychic experiences and processes connecting the present to intergenerational dynamics. They constitute a complex narrative structure of images, behaviors, and rituals that generate what phantom narratives are archetypal stories told through a myriad of collective and individual expressions of how the unconscious expresses these overlapping dynamics of the group and the individual within a historical process.

Cultural complexes are collective and cumulative; they involve social suffering; and they express themselves in a wide variety of individual and group symptoms including anxiety, depression, and acting out in various ways. They are also manifested in a variety of social conditions like poverty, crime, marginalization, group oppression, ongoing persecution, and discrimination expressed over many generations.

The four-hundred-year intergenerational story for African Americans begins with the Africans taken into slavery and brought to the United States in chains, through the Jim Crow period and its overt aggressions, racism, and race-based segregation – all expressions of the systemic results of racism. These are not only forms of social terrorism but also how the unconscious expressed its responses to trauma, violence, violation, and oppression.

Black Lives Matter movement as an expression of a phantom narrative

The impetus for this example comes from my attempts to make sense of the ongoing cultural phenomena wherein a relatively large number of African American and brown-skinned young male citizens, many unarmed, are shot by police officers. Many of these incidents have been captured on body cameras and cellphones and reported by numerous observers. In reviewing some of these incidents (phenomena), we can see right away several responses and two narratives forming. From the point of view of the *first narrative*, these events are structured as crime and punishment. This narrative tends to leave out, or not acknowledge, the emotional and social forces that are expressions of a far larger intergenerational, cultural narrative of blatant cultural racism in the form of police brutality. This brutality is enacted under the guise of tough-on-crime laws (such as stop and frisk), which should be applied equally to all Americans, but is actually an expression of a *dual legal system* (*second narrative*) that has evolved from the legacy of racism in the United States. According to this *second narrative*, race allowed us to avoid the trade-off between society's "demand" to get tough on crime and its "demand" to retain civil liberties, through unequal enforcement of the laws. In essence, tying crime to observable characteristics (such as race or religious affiliation) allowed the majority to pass tough-on-crime policies without having to bear the full burden of these policies, permitting these laws and attitudes to be sustained over time. Thus, the history of racism colors our perceptions of race and crime. The criminal justice system (as seen in the mass incarceration of young Black and Latino citizens) has become a kind of, as one writer called it, "welfare program for the poor," and has given rise to the rebirth of a caste system and the birth of mass incarceration (Alexander, 2012, p. 1).

> The rhetoric of "law and order" was first mobilized in the late 1950s as Southern governors and law enforcement officials attempted to generate and mobilize white opposition to the Civil Rights Movement. In the years following *Brown v. Board of Education*, civil rights activists used direct-action tactics in an effort to force reluctant Southern states to desegregate public facilities. Southern governors and law enforcement officials often characterized these tactics as criminal and argued that the rise of the Civil Rights Movement was indicative of a breakdown of law and order.
>
> (Alexander, 2012, p. 1)

Alexander goes on to report there are more African American men in the prison system (prison, jail, on parole or probation) than were enslaved in 1850. More recently, this racial caste system has been beefed up through the war on drugs, which gave rise to an underclass of incarcerated people of color. Thus, the crime and punishment, tough on crime, law and order narrative, as seen from an alternative point of view, expresses the organization of power structures, injustice, racial discrimination, and racial fantasies.

A brief look at some statistics from Statistica (an online statistics, market research, and business intelligence portal) provides context for my reflections:

- Police killed at least 102 unarmed Black people in 2015; 37 percent of unarmed people killed by police in 2015 were Black.
- Only 9 of the 102 cases resulted in officers being charged with a crime.
- And in 2016, 258 Black men were killed; 39 of these men were unarmed.

This is clearly disproportionate, as Black men make up 6 percent of the US population. Race seems to be a trigger for police brutality as well as other microaggressions and oppressions. Statistics for the past three years continue to express the disproportionate application of lethal force by police officers. Statistics for 2017, 2018, and 2019 are shown in Table 4.1.

Table 4.1 Number of people shot to death by the police in the United States from 2017 to 2019

	2017	2018	2019
Whites	457	223	54
Blacks*	399	209	204
Hispanics	312	205	197

Source: Statistica (2021).

* Blacks are 13 percent of the population.

The legal standard that guides the courts in dealing with these matters rarely holds these officers accountable. Courts have reasoned that the essential basis of police work requires that they act (instantly) on a situation where they perceive (react to?) an issue of danger to themselves and/or to public safety. Instinctive reactions were the final arbitrator for guilt or innocence. That is to say, *how the officer saw the situation or experienced the danger is the baseline.*

However, when we view videos of these events, many of us see something that goes against common sense – the victim is walking away from the officer, or the victim is lying face down on the ground, or the victim is shot multiple times in instances of overkill. When placed side by side – the crime and punishment narrative and commonsense perception – I am left with the experience that something unexplained and unseen is happening in plain sight.

To quote the relational psychoanalyst Philip Bromberg, who helped me think more deeply about this situation: "By living together in the enacted shadow of what is visible but not perceived, an opportunity is afforded to encounter what has been hidden in plain sight" (Bromberg, 2013, p. 1). To hear Bromberg's comments from the point of view of dissociative states of mind operating at both the individual, group, and cultural levels, we can imagine that within these states of mind our ability to reflect on our own, the other, and the context in which we are situated is compromised by an emotional field that, I feel, is organized by cultural complexes. The effects of unconscious activities of cultural complex dynamics haunt and entangle us in all manner of psychosocial dynamics. James Hollis, in his book *Hauntings: Dispelling the Ghosts Who Run Our Lives* (2013), develops the theme around how unconscious complexes function as presences that run our lives. Returning to the title of this chapter, then, "Unbearable Things,

Unseen," mentioned by Morrison, may be experienced psychologically as unconscious complexes or as ghosts pushing us toward personal and cultural consciousness.

In their paper "The Police, Black and Hispanic Boys: A Dangerous Inability to Mentalize," Kirkland Vaughans and Lisa Harris

> explore the contemporary socially toxic situation between Black and Hispanic male youth and police officers from both a historical perspective and through the lens of the psychoanalytic concept of mentalization. As a result of the failure to mentalize Black and Hispanic male youth they are not depicted as vulnerable or in need of guidance and support but rather their behavior is quickly criminalized resulting in a punitive social response. The authors conclude that effective change warrants multiple systems to address this situation, including mental health, education, criminal justice system, as well as the creation of employment opportunities.
>
> (2016, p. 171)

In exploring these "toxic" processes, we reveal our unconscious projections as they concretize the dynamics that make up the experience/expression of unconscious meanings. As we open to looking at our projections, we enter the area Luz Calvo called the primal scene of miscegenation, which he says is "a psychic structure that organizes a subject's relationship to the other through fantasies of inter-racial sexuality" (2008, p. 57). In other words, given the historical trauma that white and Black people are embroiled in, their automatic responses, that is, their instinctive responses, are pre-shaped by the historical situation that they find themselves in today. The context is the many undigested and unworked-through histories that started with slavery from Africa to the United States to Jim Crow (separate but equal structures that included social stratification). They reflect the kinds of polarities and opposites that have defined our struggles with race.

The felt sense that something else is happening raises several questions: what is this other thing going on and what do we do with our feelings and reactions to what we are seeing? What do officers see? Who do they see? What are the culture's attitudes that are expressed in these events? Which part of what we see do we identify with? Which narrative? What's the phantom narrative? Is the unseen and enacted shadow the unarticulated story?

I suggest these questions and the responses of officers, victims, witnesses, and media viewers are structured by cultural complexes, and they invite us to look for the contribution of collective shadow processes that seem to generate these deep instinctive reactions to threat and danger. Racial subjugation and oppression, and victims and perpetrators, operate within our stratified society.

To further translate the previous statement into psychological language, we could say that what is seen in the interactions of police officers and Black men is a complex racial fantasy structure that is generated within a social/political context grounded in differences and otherness, power and sexuality. These dynamics are managed through projections, splitting, and denial. This is a dynamism wherein outer forms disappear and become represented in a different form (fantasies) associated with, to use alchemical language, the *Nigredo*. These fantasies are largely the product of the unconscious psyche, which are organized by cultural complexes expressing shadow dynamics. These processes are the essential themes in the movie *Get Out* (2017), directed by Jordan Peele.

Get Out – what do they see?

In this 2017 movie, a young white female and a young Black male go to meet her parents, who live a rather sumptuous lifestyle. From the very start of the movie, the viewer is pulled into a kind of anticipatory anxiety, which runs counter to the well-manicured scenery of place and family. Our anticipatory anxiety begins to haunt the movie, as we wonder about what may happen and, to everyone's surprise, does happen, but beyond expectations. Peele calls the movie both a social thriller and a horror film. It is told through the anxiety of the Black character's emergent anxiety within a social situation that gave me the creeps. I experienced the visceral-level communication that is in the background of this interracial encounter.

Peele is well aware of the underlying anxiety ("instinctive reactions") that these scenes evoke. The character's reactions as well as our own are structured intersubjectively by a cultural history connected to race, that is, by cultural complexes. Ken Hardy, African American psychologist, speaks of

> symptoms ranging from hopelessness to acting out behavior. Racial oppression is seldom seen as contributing to these difficulties, and discussions of race are dismissed as manufacturing excuses, justifying bad behavior. As with other forms of trauma, we ask the wrong questions about youth of color. Instead of what is wrong, we need to ask the trauma informed question, "What happened to them?"
>
> (2013, p. 25)

Michelle Alexander, in her work *The New Jim Crow: Mass Incarceration in the Age of Colorblindness* (2010), speaks to the conflict between the ideas of "Black Lives Matter" and "All Lives Matter." It's critical to acknowledge the specificity of America's racial history and its contribution to the suffering of Black people today, she says. And, at the same time, we need to build bridges between communities and recognize how their issues and problems intersect.

What do they see? This brings up the question of projection. What distorts the perception, throwing off adaptation to the situation, clouding judgment? Jung defines projection as intentional, unconscious transfer of subjective aspects into the other (1971, para. 783). Unlike a simple mistake in perception that can be corrected by new information, projection in the sense in which Jung utilizes it finds that the projector defends him- or herself against the new or different information coming in. There is a lot at stake in this way of looking at projection.

This was brought home to me when on my morning drive to my office I was slowed down by a large moving van in front of me. A large warning sign was painted on the back in bold letters: "If you don't see my mirrors, I can't see you." Consciously, I thought the sign was meant to alert those drivers behind or wanting to pass the truck about the large blind spot created by the locations of the mirrors and the back of the truck. My second thought was, "What a statement about the invisibility of our process of projections!" When we don't see the other, the other cannot see us. And even when we do see and are seen, it is never a direct encounter; it is always by way of a mirror, the lenses of our own and the other's subjectivity. This is a tragic reality, for the mutuality of seeing and being seen is the process by which observer and observed, self and other, create an intersubjective context for psychic life. The wisdom on the back of the moving van was ominous and perhaps reflective of the present difficulty with face-to-face seeing and I-thou encounters, expressing less an eternal verity than the cynical ideology of the current cultural complex (Kimbles, 2014, p. 229).

We have gotten to the beginning of an answer to the question, *What do they see?* We are dealing with projections, both personal and cultural. The space created by these projections involving racial relations shows up in the shadow of the visible – "in plain sight" (Bromberg, 2013, p. 1).

Over the past few years several films have featured African themes: *Hidden Figures, Get Out, Moonlight, Thirteen,* and a documentary film, *I Am Not Your Negro,* featuring the author and activist James Baldwin who, in his own way, speaks to the profound activation of projective identification in racial relations. I highlight some of the key aspects of this interview with Baldwin that I feel point to his awareness of and his speaking to the processes related to racialized projections:

> That what you say about somebody else, anybody else, reveal you. What I think of you as being comes out of my own necessity, psychology, fears and desires. I am not talking about you when I describe you. I'm describing me. Now here in this country we have something called a nigger. It doesn't exist in any other countries in the world. We invented the nigger. I didn't invent him. White people invented him. That had to be rooted in you. Something you were afraid of. You invested me with it. If that's so. I know this and I've always known, really always, and that's part of the agony, I am not a nigger. But if I am not the nigger. And if it's true you created it. Who is the nigger? I am not the victim here. But still think, I gather, a nigger is necessary to you. I give your problem back. You're the nigger baby. It's not me.

> (Peck, 2016)

To deconstruct Baldwin's statement, he has developed or generated an awareness that grows out of a sense of marginalization and alienation in relationship to being Black in America – an attitude toward racism that allowed him to see the kinds of projections that Black people have been pushed to carry. He said, "It is painful, I know this and I've always known, really always, and that's part of the agony." It is easy for me, and I imagine for many readers, to identify on a conscious level what constitutes some of these images of the other.

The kind of projections that Baldwin's questions point to are the kinds of group-level psychic manifestations of fear and anxiety that are at the core of racial projections. These inevitably express forms, figures, and presences (cultural phantoms) that carry the fears, hopes, and identity needs derived from breakdowns in tradition and disruptions in our life/societal continuity.

How do we see that we do not see? How do we question our comfortable stance that we are innocent? An alchemical dictum says, "Dissolve the matter in its own water." The process in alchemy takes place in the *Nigredo* – the blackness of not seeing, not recognizing, and not understanding. The projective processes I am referring to implicate all of us. We are in it. Can we see and locate ourselves in what we see?

I feel that analytical psychology's role in cultural and political affairs is to help elaborate our understanding of and relationship to cultural processes as they play themselves out in psychological and cultural life. Cultural complexes and projective defenses (images) are powerful players in the generation of phantom narratives that serve as counterpoints to received history and social policy. These narratives express drives toward the need for recognition and urges against death and annihilation expressed in social structures and policies that produce non-recognition.

In our moral crisis, the question is how to transform collective processes, how to understand our own group process in a way that facilitates a consciousness that contributes to group development through the recognition of and work with presences in the collective unconscious and of the unconscious in the collective. Through examples from society and film, I have elucidated the processes that manifest through the various presences in psychological life that must be engaged for political and global change to occur.

In the Richard Wilhelm translation of the *I Ching*, Hexagram 21, Biting Through, six in the third place says:

> Six in the third place means:
> Bites on old dried meat
> And strikes on something poisonous.
> Slight humiliation. No blame.

The commentary:

> Punishment is to be carried out by someone who lacks the power and authority to do so. Therefore, the culprits do not submit. The matter at issue is an old one – as symbolized by salted game – and in dealing with its difficulties arise. This old meat is spoiled: by taking up the problem the punisher arouses poisonous hatred against himself, and in this way is put in a somewhat humiliating position. But since punishment was required by the time, he remains free of blame.
>
> (1968, p. 86)

Psychologically, the process of dealing with cultural traumas and violence grows out of the othering of differences.

In the case of racial relations, Isaac Balbus, writing about reparation, says:

> the racial fantasy structure ... prevents whites from relating to blacks. Thus, whites who inhabit this racial fantasy world are defended

against the racial analogue of depressive anxiety and guilt – that is, from the sorrow and remorse that would otherwise accompany the realization that they have harmed the blacks they love.

(2005, p. 111)

In closing, I offer you a poem by Wendell Berry (2012), who seems to have taken up the issue of his responsibility to the harm that has been done through racism.

My Great-grandfather's Slaves

Deep in the back ways of my mind I see them
going in the long days
over the same fields that I have gone
long days over.

I see the sun passing and burning high
over that land from their day
until mine, their shadow
having risen and consumed them.

I see them obeying and watching
the bearded tall man whose voice
and blood is mine, whose countenance
in stone at his grave my own resembles
whose blindness is my brand.

I see them kneel and pray to the white God
Who buys their souls with Heaven.

I see them approach, quiet
In the merchandise of their flesh,
To put down their burdens
of firewood and hemp and tobacco
into the minds of my kinsmen.

I see them moving in the rooms of my history
the day of my birth entering
the horizon emptied of their days,
their purchased lives taken back
into the dust of birthright.

I see them borne, shadow within shadow,
shroud within shroud, through all nights
from their lives to mine, long beyond
reparation or given liberty
or any straightness.

I see them go in the bonds of my blood
through all the time of their bodies.

I have seen that freedom cannot be taken
from one man and given to another,
and cannot be taken and kept.

I know that freedom can only be given,
And is the gift to the giver
from the one who receives.

I am owned by the blood of all of them
whoever were owned by my blood,
We cannot be free of each other

References

Alexander, M. (2010). *The new Jim Crow: Mass incarceration in the age of colorblindness*. New York, NY: The New Press.

Alexander, M. (2012). The new Jim Crow. In *Mass incarceration as a form of racialized social control*. Teaching Tolerance, Southern Poverty Law Center. Retrieved from www.tolerance.org/classroom-resources/tolerance-lessons/mass-incarceration-as-a-form-of-racialized-social-control

Balbus, I. (2005). The psychodynamics of racial reparations. In *Mourning and modernity: Essays in the psychoanalysis of contemporary society* (pp. 91–115). New York: Other Press.

Berry, W. (2012). My great-grandfather's slaves. In *New collected poems*. Berkeley, CA: Counterpoint Press.

Bromberg, P. (2013). Hidden in plain sight: Thoughts on imagination and the lived unconscious. *Psychoanalytic Dialogues, 23*, 1–14.

Calvo, L. (2008). Racial fantasies and the primal scene of miscegenation. *International Journal of Psychoanalysis, 89*(1), 55–78.

Hardy, K. (2013). Healing the wounds of racial trauma. *Reclaiming Journal, 22*(1), 24–28. Retrieved from https://static1.squarespace.com/static/545cdfcce4b0a64725b9f65a/t/54da3451e4b0ac9bd1d1cd30/1423586385564/Healing.pdf

Hollis, J. (2013). *Dispelling the ghosts who run our lives.* Asheville, NC: Chiron Publications.

Jung, C. G. (1968). The meaning of psychology for modern man (1933/1934). In *The collected works of C.G. Jung: Vol. 10. Civilization in transition.* Princeton, NJ: Princeton University Press.

Jung, C. G. (1969). The relations between the ego and the unconscious (1928). In *The collected works of C.G. Jung: Vol. 7. Two essays on analytical psychology.* Princeton, NJ: Princeton University Press.

Jung, C. G. (1971). *The collected works of C.G. Jung: Vol. 6. Psychological types.* Princeton, NJ: Princeton University Press.

Kimbles, S. (2014). *Phantom narratives: The unseen contributions from culture to psyche.* Lanham, MD: Rowland and Littlefield Publishing Group.

Layton, L. (2008). Relational thinking: From culture to couch and couch to culture. In S. Clarke, H. Hahn, & P. Hoggett (Eds.), *Object relations and social relations: The implications of the relational turn in psychoanalysis* (pp. 1–24). London: Karnac Books.

Morrison, T. (1989). Unspeakable things, unspoken: The Afro-American presence in American literature. *Michigan Quarterly Review, 28*(1), 1–34. http://hdl.handle.net/2027/spo.act2080.0028.001:01

Odajnyk, V. W. (1976). *Jung and politics: The political and social ideas of C.G. Jung.* New York, NY: Harper and Row.

Peck, R. (Director). (2016). *I am not your negro* [Documentary]. Based on *Remember this house,* by James Baldwin. United States: Magnolia Pictures, Amazon Studios.

Peele, J. (Director). (2017). *Get out* [Motion picture]. United States: Universal Pictures.

Statistica. (2021) Number of people shot to death by the police in the United States from 2017 to 2019, by race. Retrieved from www.statista.com/statistics/585152/people-shot-to-death-by-us-police-by-race/

Vaughans, K. C., & Harris, L. (2016). The police, Black and Hispanic boys: A dangerous inability to mentalize. *Journal of Infant, Child, and Adolescent Psychotherapy, 15*(3), 171–178.

Wilhelm, R. (1968). *The I Ching, or book of changes.* Princeton, NJ: Princeton University Press.

Chapter 5

Phantom narratives and the uncanny in cultural life

Psychic presences and their shadows

> There is another world, but it is in this one.
>
> Paul Éluard[1]

In this chapter I focus on the emotional factors that are activated at the level of the cultural unconscious, producing experiences of the uncanny through phantom narratives, expressions of the unconscious at the level of the group, appearing as individual, social, and cultural dynamics. As mentioned previously, the concept of the cultural unconscious was introduced to analytical psychology by Joseph Henderson (1990), who defined it as "an area of historical memory that lies between the collective unconscious and the manifest patterns of the culture" (p. 103). It may include these modalities – both consciously and unconsciously – but it derives some kind of uncanny identity arising from the archetypes of the collective unconscious, which, just as they assist in the formation of myth and ritual, also promote the process of acculturative development in individuals (p. 190).

Additionally, I will apply Jung's concept of complexes to cultural processes that appear as cultural complexes. Complexes are naturally occurring elements in human beings that structure individual responses to biological givens such as the body, aging, and death, and to interpersonal relations within familial, tribal, and broader communal systems. These naturally occurring elements are organized through affective dynamics that are often unconscious. They are the psyche's way of narrating its relationship to the group. Hence, basic cultural issues of invisibility, namelessness, marginalization, powerlessness, and rootlessness are existential issues facing all of us. When these issues are linked up with losses, racism, gender, and ethnicity, the psychology of differences comes into play along with power dynamics, as group survival seems to be at stake. Cultural complexes serve the need to belong and have an identity by linking group expectations with personal experiences. These complex dynamics tend to function in the emotional background but assume a certain importance and influence nonetheless as they express emotional valences for the group and the individual (Kimbles, 2014; Singer & Kimbles, 2004).

Thus, an understanding of cultural complexes allows us to understand our emotions, beliefs, and images that operate at the level of the group and contribute to the organization of group phenomena. I see cultural complexes as the *bones* (structures) of cultural processes and phantom narratives as the *flesh* (lived experiences) of cultural experiences. In this respect, Jung puts forth a nonrational life force as the center of the human psyche:

> If we look back into the past history of mankind, we find among many other religious convictions, a universal belief in the existence of phantoms or ethereal beings who dwell in the neighborhood of men and who exercise an invisible yet powerful influence upon them
>
> (Jung, 1981, para. 570)

The uncanny

Freud says in the opening of his paper on the uncanny, "Only rarely does the psychoanalyst feel impelled to engage in 'aesthetic investigations'" (1919, p. 123). Later, he acknowledges that the term belongs to the realm of the frightening, of what evokes fear and dread . . . but presumes an "affective nucleus," which justifies the use of a special conceptual term.

I see in Freud's use of the term "affective nucleus" both a phantom echo of Jung's theory of complexes and recognition of the transpersonal emotional core of many cultural complexes. Freud based his analysis of the uncanny on E.T.A. Hoffmann's text *Der Sandmann*, which led him to explore a number of etymological features of the term *unheimlich*, ostensibly the opposite of *heimlich* – a transition from the familiar (*heimlich*) to the unfamiliar (*unheimlich*), and yet fully retaining its connection to what in the cultural life of a family one has once more consciously known. *Unheimlich* (unfamiliar), although associated with the self and known to the self yet supposed to remain hidden from the self, has become apparent, has become visible to the self. "The unheimlich, though unfamiliar, comes bundled with references to the self" (Rahimi, 2013, p. 459).

As for Freud's conclusion about the uncanny, he says: "We have to admit that none of this helps us to understand the extraordinarily strong feelings of something uncanny that pervades that conception" (1919, p. 236). He concludes that the origin of the uncanny is castration and the return of the repressed – the uncanny tropes are a group of phenomena "in which the frightening element can be shown to be something repressed which returns" (p. 241).

The concept of the uncanny has moved far beyond Freud's understanding of it as representing the continued presence of animism, omnipotence of thought based on it, and repressed infantile complexes. It is now used as a key concept to grasp the experience of political and social alienation resulting from uprootedness, disturbing unhomeliness (not just for refugees and immigrants). It is under these circumstances that the familiar becomes uncanny and frightening. We saw an example of this in 2001, when, in the aftermath of 9/11, the terror of invasion and attack led to widespread political fear in the United States, leading to a "War on Terror," conspiracy theories, fear of weapons of mass destruction, and the need for more control and repression at the expense of civil liberties. Cultural changes, whether expressed through sudden political responses or long-standing historical traumas such as slavery, can produce in our individual psyches disturbing feelings that alienate us from the familiar social world of others, both familiar and unfamiliar.

Later literature on the uncanny

The literature used to speak about the uncanny is replete with images that range from *doppelgangers*, alter egos, and splits to ghosts, unsettling doubling, madness, and invasive phantoms. Though Freud interpreted the uncanny on the personal level as due to castration anxiety and infantile complexes similarly rooted in the force of early developmental issues, others have expanded its definition. For instance, Sadeq Rahimi writes:

> It is also useful to consider the place of mirrors and the visual in the historical trajectory of the modern conceptions of human selfhood. This role is worth attention for two reasons: the triangular relationship between the visual, the ego and the uncanny, and the social and historical embeddedness of the experience of subjectivity.
>
> (2013, p. 455)

I extend the meaning of the uncanny to social and cultural processes *operating at the level of the cultural unconscious*. Avery Gordon's

(2008) reframing of the uncanny in social terms is consistent with my view of the uncanny:

> The social is ultimately what the uncanny is about: *being haunted in the world of common reality*. To be haunted is not a contest between animism and a discrediting reality test, nor a contest between the unconscious and the conscious faculties. It is an enchanted encounter in a disenchanted world between familiarity and strangeness.
>
> (pp. 54–55)

To my mind, Gordon's use of "haunting" is quite cognate with Freud's notion of the uncanny. The recognition that a social phenomenon is involved moves repression through stages of a culture's troubled past, from suppression of "alternative histories" to oppressed peoples' generation of new stories and finally (and more bleakly) to "alienation as an economic, political, psychological and existential condition" (Masschelein, 2011, p. 136).

Phantoms and their narratives

I introduced the concept of *phantom narratives* as a hybridized term linking personal and social realms of unconscious story formation, expressing the background ambiguity of subject/object, individual/group, politics/sociology, and personal biography and cultural history, conscious and unconscious, held together in an affective field. This affective field has a narrative structure that operates at the level of the cultural unconscious and is, along with particular images, at the very heart of cultural complexes, drawing unconscious attention to unprocessed cultural history. Phantoms as images are representations at the core of these complexes, and their narratives give the complexes their dynamic agency.

Looked at from within the context of the cultural unconscious, cultural complexes, phantom narratives, and the uncanny are expressions of disruptions in the unconscious at the group or cultural level of the psyche into the world of both individual and social and/or cultural reality. These disruptions affect roles, ideologies, and societal structures, while disturbing our subjective orientation – the order of things. Parallel disruptions occur at every level of psychological and sociological functioning.

In a recent movie, *Phoenix* (2014), directed by Christian Petzold, we get a representation of a weaving together of the personal life of a woman, post-concentration camp, within the context of post-World War II Nazi destruction. As the movie opens, a disfigured, bandaged woman (Nelly) is returning to Berlin for reconstructive surgery. She wants to have her original face back, even though it has been damaged during her concentration camp ordeal. She says, "I want to look exactly like I used to." She is a traumatized and shattered woman who also returns to track down her husband, who may have betrayed her Jewish background to the Nazis. He was released and she was placed in a concentration camp.

She returns to the Phoenix café where she previously performed with her husband – he as the pianist and she as a singer. The husband fails to recognize Nelly but finally wants her instead ("I want you to play my wife") so that he can collect her unclaimed money. Nelly cooperates with his scheme as a way to get her identity back and to be recognized by her husband as some kind of partner again, especially since he is willing to share with her the fortune that he imagines to be that of a now dead woman. It is not until the end of the film that Johnny, the husband, is shocked into trying to make sense of the inescapable fact that this woman, his wife, has returned from the dead, at least as her spirit, even though no one has allowed her to be herself. She has, in effect, become the phantom of her own culturally repressed past.

Looked at from the point of view of phantoms and narratives, the pair has lost everything, including the ability to each grant an authentic identity to the other. The reconstructive wish for a return to a previous identity so that life can be resumed as it was (Nelly) or started anew (Johnny) is played out against the historical weight of a narrative of catastrophic destruction (the loss of everything). Thus, the film offers a vivid picture of living in a world that has all the features of the uncanny, particularly the doubling of identity, the confusion between being alive and the living dead-like existence that characterizes such extreme dislocation – the clear line of distinction is lost. The breakdown of the denial that Nelly and Johnny share, and the vague recognition of someone previously known but who is now a stranger, constitute the denouement – a moment that is uncanny.

Anneleen Masschelein in her book *The Unconcept* gives a description of the uncanny that is close to mine:

> The uncanny is a key concept to grasp the experience of aesthetic estrangement, political and social alienation resulting in a deeply rooted, disturbing of unhomeliness that characterizes human existence in the world but tempered by a mild, surrealistic undertones and the guise of familiarity.

(2011, p. 147)

In a similar way to Masschelein, I feel the phantom narrative is a basic concept that allows an imaginative way to articulate the experience of the uncanny as it manifests itself in individual and group history within the context of cultural dynamics.

Phantom narratives

Phantom narratives are the unconscious operating at the group level, narrating themselves in the midst of cultural complexes as psychic presences of great fascination and uncanny power. What is "uncanny" in the phantom narratives grows out of an affective field "with deep and buried contents," ideas of deep structures in language (Chomsky, 1968).

James Grotstein's understanding of "psychic presences" helps to amplify the term *phantom*, first introduced by Nicolas Abraham and Maria Torok (1994), although without the notion of narrative that Grotstein manages to imply:

> My term psychic presences are meant to convey the experience of intrapsychic preternatural entities, which present as images or phantoms and which we, in turn, reify as real. These images of phantoms undergo a transfiguration of transmogrifications as we progress . . . they evolve into symbolic images that designate the "presence of the absence" of the object-person, that is, the presence of the legacy of the experience with the object in its absence.
>
> (Grotstein, 2000, p. xix)

By linking "psychic presences" and "phantoms" with a notion of their "narratives," I propose a way of opening up an imaginative space for reflecting on the changes and impacts that our current historical situation, with its "too muchness" and disorientation, brings to us as context and content for adaptation and engagement.

Phantom narratives encode the representations of psychic presences in dynamic stories that quite literally narrate the individual's relationship to the group and group life, on the one hand, and the accompanying context that gives each phantomatic figure its meaning, on the other (the "phantom narrative" is the intergenerational story placed in the context of its central image). Here, I would like to elaborate my understanding of the relationship between a phantom narrative and the uncanny with a personal example, a dream I had a number of years ago when in advanced candidacy of Jungian analytical training.

> *I am called to be a consultant at a meeting of three staff psychologists at a prison. Present at the meeting are three African American men, all psychologists working in the prison system. The three men I identify as a colleague from graduate school, the first president of the American Black Psychologists Association, and a man who was a combination of my father and Clarence Thomas (Associate Justice of the Supreme Court). I am being asked to consult around a problem the group is grappling with, which is that although mental health services have been made available and given to the Black community and prisoners, the rate of young Black men being imprisoned remains extremely high. The psychologists have no useful explanation for this situation. They think that as an analytical psychologist I may have something to offer from an archetypal psychology point of view.*

Let me give some of my conscious experience with these three men. The first, the colleague from graduate school, was trained in humanistic psychology and at the time of my dream was a professor at a local university. The second man had been connected with the creation of the Association of Black Psychologists, formed "in recognition of the diverse historical experiences and cultural expressions within and between peoples of African ancestry" (ABPsi, 2015). The third man was a combination of my father and Clarence Thomas, a member of the US Supreme Court known for his relatively conservative views. Paradoxically, Thomas as a Black justice replaced Thurgood Marshall, an active liberal attorney best known for his argument before the Supreme Court that the separate but equal doctrine was unconstitutional. Later, Marshall was appointed an associate justice to the Supreme Court, the first African American to hold that position. My father, though conservative around racial matters like Thomas, emphasized and mirrored, like Marshall, the importance and role of racial pride.

My dream presents a complicated subgroup of African American men, all psychologists, who represent a range of attitudes toward racial mental health, but they felt something was missing in their approach, for nothing they came up with could help stem the tide of the continued incarceration of young African American men. They needed to find out from me what an archetypal attitude could add to their work. All three men focused on aspects of structural violence as manifested in economic disparity in opportunity, social and political power (privileges), and the effects of these disparities on mental health issues that show up as problems of crime.

Though I had my dream two decades ago, the continued rate of imprisonment of African American males have earned the United States the descriptive term *mass incarceration* (see Alexander, 2010; Cox, 2015). The statistics referred to in an article by Robyn Cox (2015, p. 5) and cited by Ta-Nehisi Coates (2015) are staggering. The United States has the highest incarceration rate in the world; although it has 5 percent of the world's population, it houses about 25 percent of the world's prisoners. It incarcerates a Black male 20 to 50 times longer than a white prisoner convicted of the same drug crime. Two and a third million men are incarcerated – about half for drug crimes. Seventy percent of men imprisoned are Black and Hispanic. There are seven million Americans, males and females, either in prison, on parole, or on probation, mostly for selling drugs.

Professor Cox argues in her article, "Mass Incarceration and the Struggle for Civil Rights":

> It is clear that crime and punishment are multidimensional problems that stem from racial prejudice justified by age-old perceptions and beliefs about African Americans. . . . Public policy, criminal justice actors, society and the media, and criminal behavior have all played roles in creating what sociologist Loie Wacquant calls the hyper incarceration of black men.
>
> (2015, p. 2)

And later in the same article she says:

> Failure to address the legacy of racism passed down by our forefathers and its ties to economic oppression will only result in the continued reinvention of Jim Crow . . . from this point of view the penal system could be viewed as an extension of chattel slavery.
>
> (p. 3)

Psychologically, this would mean turning the Other into an object to be owned.

Though quite disturbing, Cox's conclusions appear to have continued the approach of the psychologists in my dream that occurred two decades ago. She does add the intergenerational transmission of unconscious racism (cultural complexes). As my own dream was a generation ago, I find it sad that the same dynamics that troubled my African American psychologist colleagues continue to this present day.

The uncanny and phantom narratives

Although some psychologists and sociologists have adopted a psycho-social approach to the problems addressed in my dream, considering the dream through the lens of phantom narratives allows me to look at a psycho-emotional-archetypal approach to the complicated intersection of individual, cultural, and historical dynamics from the point of view of the activity of the unconscious at the level of the group, as expressed by cultural complexes. Although we are likely to focus on scapegoating and splitting as operating in intergroup relations, the processes, fears, fantasies, and feelings that give rise to the need for these emotional processes are rarely explored. From the point of view of phantom narratives, group experiences of cultural processes are manifested in figures and images that structure both intra-psychic and intersubjective aspects of experiencing that bring into play cultural history, social context, beliefs, and values that affectively shape group and individual responses to these cultural and social issues.

As an imagined consultation, through my dream, this chapter is an expression of another of many actual and symbolic consultations I have made in response to my dream, putting to me the question of what archetypal psychology has to offer to this large social and cultural problem of race relations as it manifests in the problem of mass incarceration of young African American men in the United States. By bringing together some of my thoughts on phantom narratives and Freud's ideas around the uncanny as these relate to cultural, social, and political issues, I hope to open up an imaginative space for the role of affect and images to be encountered as expressions of the dynamics of those aspects of the unconscious that link psyche and culture.

Although I have focused on African American men, the same dynamics (scapegoating, denial of group and individual shadow, splitting) that we find in their mass incarceration are easily identifiable within other cultural groups struggling to achieve a successful relationship to American identity after an early cultural history elsewhere (for instance, the large group of young, underemployed Latino men).

The image of the phantom haunts narratives that relate individuals to the group and the group to the individual, opening up an encounter with the uncanny at the level of the cultural unconscious. The phantom narrative shows what is undigested but still important in the past of a culture and how significant and emotionally alive it continues to be, both for the individual and the group that shares this past. Cultural complexes organize such narratives, but their central phantomatic images give a specifically uncanny thrust to them. I propose that a phantom narrative constitutes the unconscious (at the level of the group) way of expressing in symbolic form what it is doing with the experience of social and political alienation. Bollas's term, the "unthought known" (1987), aptly expresses the implicit stories that organize inter- and intra-group relating. The cultural unconscious is structured by units of experience (cultural complexes) where individual, group, and societal processes affectively come together in a tangled web of cultural, psychic, and group processes that are lived out subjectively and intersubjectively. Phantom narratives are structures of images, behaviors, and rituals that give notice to the "social nature of the subjective life" of the group and the individual relationship to the group through various social and ritual forms (see Gordon, 2008). It is one way to understand the expression at the unconscious level of the group. The organization of group processes as cultural complexes refuses to accept our understanding of history as a simple linearity, opening up a space between received history and alternative narratives. The phantom fills that space with a dynamic image of a past that refuses to accept a future that does not include it. This is how, and why, it is so uncanny.

Groups that have been marginalized and traumatized through social oppression and disenfranchisement, such that there is a history of broken continuity and group fragmentation, give birth both to phantom narratives and lives that are profoundly influenced by the uncanny. The activation of phantom narratives as "phantomatic complexes" operates in what Turner (1966) has defined as a liminal space, which we might speak of here as a place between accepted cultural narratives. Phantom narratives refer to the affectively organized units of experience-patterns that organize the experiencing of the other when the other has been denied a place in narratives endorsed by the culture's conscious establishment. Phantom narratives, like cultural complexes, are "repetitive, resisting consciousness and collecting experiences that confirms their historical point of view" (Kimbles, 2014, p. 5; Singer & Kimbles, 2004, p. 6). They are traumatic images that have not been forgotten that encode, in the force of their uncanniness, only partly repressed "historical group experiences that have taken root in the cultural unconscious of the group" (see Singer & Kimbles, 2004, p. 6). As we have seen, this is where they gather life and narrative force.

Summary comments

Putting together phantom narratives and cultural complexes creates another hybrid term: *phantomatic complexes*. This term allows themes of presence and absence, visibility and invisibility, and life and death to be seen as manifestations of themes related to cultural history and trauma (inheritance and memories from past generations) to both find a voice and an imaginal expression, for instance, Hiroshima, World War II and Japan's defeat, the Holocaust in Germany, slavery in the United States, genocide around the world, and most recently the tsunami in Fukushima. All this makes for a haunting – the work of processing and dealing with these tragedies as they manifest at the unconscious level through phantomatic complexes. Phantomatic complexes are major expressions in modern cultural life of unprocessed traumatic history.

As symbolic processes, phantomatic complexes, I suggest, emerge from a variety of actual and symbolic social deaths (Patterson, 1982, pp. 7–14) that emerge out of the processes of social negation. The prototype of every other social negation is slavery. People are uprooted, deracinated, placed in a world of a master-dominated relationship, "a world of non-being" – history is broken, cultural holding is fragmented, and historical alternatives are rendered mute (Patterson, 1982, pp. 7–14). Phantom narratives as representations of cultural complexes are organized around psychic figures and images that animate and connect the individual psyche to the group, its cultural history and heritage. They function at the cultural level of the unconscious, creating by intergenerational transmission certain tasks for future generations to perform at the individual, group, and community level. An unresolved historical event or situation emerges from repression, and a type of haunting ensues. The figures appearing in cultural complexes are phantoms and are often experienced spectrally as strange and uncanny. They are organized as phantom narratives (implicit structures) and expressed though ideologies, cultural attitudes, rituals, and moral codes.

In the clinical situation in which cultural reality is minimized or disconnected from life experiences, the individual experiences alienation and invisibility is made manifest. From this point of view, at the clinical level of transference and countertransference enactments in analysis, phantomatic complexes always influence interpretations. The analytic relationship, with its historic past, its cultural trauma, its potential for healing the patient's cultural heritage, and its potential for community healing, creates a rich phantomatic field for exploration.

I am not, however, postulating something that we cannot feel or find in our conscious emotional repertoire. I find it uncanny, for instance, that, given the relentless repetition of the phantomatic narrative of an obvious form of loss of freedom and all the associated cultural complexes that we find in the mass incarceration of young men of color, we have managed to perpetuate a former generation's blindness to the repetition of slave history into a supposedly more enlightened time, and that we refuse to accept slavery's ongoing presence in our everyday life. We choose not to see beyond the conscious, rational crime and punishment narrative, and so we do not see its phantomatic roots in slavery. However, if we follow Freud's understanding of the uncanny as an expression of our relationship to the frightening and the horrific, from *heimlich*, "homely," that which is kept out of sight, to *unheimlich*, the "disturbing," expressing the movement from familiarity to strangeness, we arrive at the labyrinth of cultural and institutional memory (Gordon, 2008, p. 7). The taken-for-granted cultural priorities, values, and ideals, and the institutional memories of violence and harm done in their name, point us to a strange disconnect – the ideal of equal justice under the law and the disparities found in racial and gender enforcement of the laws. Freud resolves the relationship between these two processes by bringing in the theory of repression: "The uncanny is in reality nothing new, or alien, but something which is familiar and old – established in the mind and which has become alienated from it only through the return of repression" (Freud, 1919, p. 399).

What does the large population of Black and Latino prisoners signify? Are these "non-persons" our newly initiated shadow population, rapidly becoming cultural phantoms, connecting us to the tortured, unworked-through history of slavery and its shadow of racism as a radical restriction of freedom? Although there is a feeling of having been here before, this is not simply a return under the guise of racism, but the presence in plain sight of persons made invisible and the invisible made visible.

The repressed returns, as Freud knew, through a haunting sense that we have been here before. In Toni Morrison's *Beloved* (1987), the invisible returns represented by the ghost of the murdered child "haunted by the insatiable longing for love" (Martinez, 2009). The refusal of contemporary middle-class American culture to acknowledge its complicity in the denial of the recognition of the needs of people of color is producing such phantoms today. In their narratives we can still find Black people whose needs, expressed through a variety of behaviors, the injured feelings related to the negative cultural attitudes toward them, have become intergenerational phantoms. Their narratives contribute in a major way to the obscene continuation of mass incarceration – a story that challenges cultural blindness as much as it is caused by it.

These ghosts bring demands for recognition and reparation. These are the phantom transmissions of an earlier generation's traumatic complexes to the contemporary American Black experience. The current outcry regarding the use of body cameras for police officers to reduce violence by allowing others to be an audience, to "Black Lives Matter," to putting up barriers to Hispanic immigration, to Muslim hatred, we are familiar with these processes but feel surprised by their reoccurrence. Although we may eventually see benefits from the use of body cameras by police officers, it is interesting to see how many of the recent killings of young Black men have been caught on camera and how the interpretations of officers and the public are seen through entirely different eyes. It truly is a problem of complex-activated perception. It is impossible to see if the eyes (perceptions) through which we see are not reflected on. As mentioned, I once saw a prominently placed sign on a large semi-truck calling attention to nearby drivers: "If you don't see my mirrors I can't see you."

There is no end to what I could summon in my own mirrors, but I would like to close with a poetic and weighty quote from Jung (1934/1954), referring to the opening words of the Dedication in *Faust*:

> "Once more you hover near me, forms and faces" – are more than just an aesthetic flourish. Like the concretism of the devil, they are an admission of the objectivity of psychic experience, a whispered avowal that this was what actually happened, not because of subjective wishes, or fears, or personal opinions, but somehow quite of itself. Naturally only a numskull thinks of ghosts, but something like a primitive numskull seems to lurk beneath the surface of our reasonable daytime consciousness.
>
> (para. 512)

Note

1 Although often attributed to Éluard, the source of the quote is in question as others have used it as well. Éluard quotes Ignaz-Vitalis Troxler who, in turn, quotes Albert Béguin, and so on.

References

ABPsi. (2015). Black/African-centered psychology. *The Association of Black Psychologists*. Retrieved from www.abpsi.org/pdf/

Abraham, N., & Torok, M. (1994). *The shell and the kernel*. Chicago, IL: University of Chicago Press.

Alexander, M. (2010). *The new Jim Crow: Mass incarceration in the area of color blindness*. New York, NY: The New Press.

Bollas, C. (1987). *The shadow of the object*. New York, NY: Columbia University Press.

Chomsky, N. Y. (1968). *Language and mind*. New York, NY: Harcourt, Brace and World.

Coates, T. N. (2015, October). The Black family in the age of mass incarceration. *The Atlantic*, pp. 60–84.

Cox, R. (2015). *Where do we go from here? Mass incarceration and the struggle for civil rights* [Executive Summary]. Economic Policy Institute, Washington, DC.

Freud, S. (1919). *The "Uncanny"* (Collected Papers). New York, NY: Basic Books Inc., First American Edition, 1959.

Gordon, A. (2008). *Ghostly matters: Haunting and the sociological imagination*. Minneapolis, MN: University of Minnesota Press.

Grotstein, J. (2000). *Who is the dreamer who dreams the dream?* Hillsdale, NJ: Analytic Press.

Henderson, J. (1990). *Shadow and self*. Wilmette, IL: Chiron Press.

Jung, C. G. (1934/1954). *The development of personality*. New York, NY: Princeton University Press.

Jung, C. G. (1981). *The structure and dynamics of the psyche*. New York, NY: Princeton University Press.

Kimbles, S. (2014). *Phantom narratives: The unseen contributions of culture to psyche*. Lanham, MD: Roman & Littlefield.

Martinez, I. (2009). Toni Morrison's *Beloved*: Slavery haunting America. *Journal of Jungian Scholarly Studies*, *4*(3), 1–28.

Masschelein, A. (2011). *The unconcept*. Albany, NY: State University of New York Press.

Morrison, T. (1987). *Beloved*. New York, NY: A Plume Book, Penguin Group.

Patterson, O. (1982). *Slavery and social death: A comparative study*. Cambridge, MA: Harvard University Press.

Petzold, C. (Director). (2014). *Phoenix* [Motion picture]. United States: Sundance Selects.

Rahimi, S. (2013). The ego, the ocular, and the uncanny: Why are metaphors of vision central in accounts of the uncanny? *The International Journal of Psychoanalysis*, *94*, 453–576.

Singer, T., & Kimbles, S. (Eds.). (2004). *The cultural complexes: Contemporary perspectives on psyche and society*. New York, NY: Routledge.

Turner, V. (1966). *The ritual process: Structure and anti-structure*. New Brunswick, NJ: Aldine Transaction.

Chapter 6

Between the world and me
Where the wild things live

Between the World and Me is the title of Ta-Nehisi Coates's (2015) evocative book in which he writes a letter to his teenage son. He tells him about the feelings, symbolism, and realities associated with being Black in America. Using the father-son relationship and its empathic bond and providing a holding context that potentially nourishes the son's sense of becoming, Coates's conversation becomes part of the initiation his son will need in order to navigate the dehumanizing and invalidating contacts he will experience in the world around being a Black man. The remarkable implication of this type of interaction is that it involves a necessary communication to prepare the son to deal with the multiple verbal and nonverbal insults he most likely will experience, from microaggressions to hate crimes.

Coates's conversation with his son parallels James Baldwin's (1963) letter to his nephew where he compares his nephew to the men in their family – Baldwin's brother and father. He tells his nephew about America's ability to destroy Black men and challenges his nephew to convert his anger due to mistreatment as a Black man into having a passionate and broad outlook on the Negro experience.

Baldwin speaks to his nephew in an attempt to help him avoid the spiritual disappointment and defeat suffered by his father and uncle and to help him deal with his anger and hurt and probable proneness to violence that is assumed to be a response to the racialized setup existing in American culture. The conversations that Coates and Baldwin describe are the conversations that most African American parents have with their teenage and young adult children about how to deal with confrontations with police officers, among others.

My use of the subtitle "Where the Wild Things Live" is a play on Maurice Sendak's children's book *Where the Wild Things Are* (1963). In Sendak's story, Max, our child protagonist, is able to put on his wolf suit and "make mischief of sorts." He is sent to his room for bad behavior but is able to use a fantasy of playing with the wild things, over which he gains control and then returns to the safety of his home. His imaginary trip takes place in a transitional space where fantasy and reality remain distinct enough that there is room for his imagination to germinate. This is symbolic play, which is an achievement that grows out of the child's ability to exist in a transitional space. According to D. W. Winnicott, this space

> is an area of experiencing, to which inner reality and external life both contribute. It is an area that is not challenged, because no claim is made on its behalf except that it shall exist as a resting-place for the individual engaged in the perpetual human task of keeping inner and outer reality separate and interrelated.
>
> (1971, pp. 1–2)

Ta-Nehisi Coates knows he cannot assume that the blessings of transitional space will be created in his son's interactions with the world, for there is very little gap between whatever the racial stereotypes and attitudes are and how he himself and his son experience themselves as persons. For Coates and his son, the world is structured by racialized phantasies that must be identified, engaged, and struggled with in order to achieve a sense of selfhood in relationship to the world. Coates urges his son to struggle:

> Struggle for the memory of your ancestors. Struggle for wisdom. . . . But do not struggle for the Dreamers. . . . Do not pin your struggle on their conversion. The Dreamers will have to learn to struggle for themselves.
>
> (2015, p. 151)

I assume the ancestors represent a deeper level of self-relating that includes and locates his son in his cultural history. The Dreamers are ones who live in their own self-created world around race.

Like many African Americans, although many of the damages that Coates's son will suffer will be overt, the vast majority will be implicitly communicated in the silent dynamics of racialized interactions, subjectivities, and intersubjectivities implicit in cultural life in the United States, where the cultural unconscious is full of tortured, unacknowledged, and unprocessed fantasies about otherness and differences. From this point of view, Ta-Nehisi Coates creates a relational space wherein he can share and communicate to his son a way to deal with the dangers and harms caused by racism. The father and son become "like subjects" (Benjamin, 1995).

Between the World and Me creates a space in which how one is perceived (and conceived, that is, constructed) is not generally based on seeing one's humanity but an object that reflects the racialized other. This is a complicated set of processes that must be sorted out. Similar to what Sendak's Max experiences, many phantasies must be engaged in the overlap of subjectivity and objectivity. Racial phantasies about who one is are as psychically real as beliefs, but function unconsciously as facts, and thus collapse transitional space and mutual recognition as "like subjects" (Benjamin, 1995).

In this chapter I invite readers to open their imagination to this place where the wild things live through examining the collective projections in our groups and in ourselves. I hope we can then see and learn about ourselves, each other, and the nature of the cultural context in which we live that contribute to the creation of wild things. I hope we can make visible the forces that operate implicitly in two areas that contribute mightily to the racialized context in our country: intergenerational dynamics and our culture's collective shadow.

How are collective processes created? Jungian analyst John Dourley (2003) gives a brief description of how he feels collective processes are created:

> All civilizations, past and present, owe their existence and endurance to social processes of archetypal bonding that are formally in their lasting cultural achievements. This bonding works a double effect. It at once legitimates the society's supremacy among societies and in so doing grounds that society's latent hatred of differently bonded societies.
>
> (p. 136)

These implicit structures and forces and stories are created around the dynamics of archetypal bonding and hatred, what I call phantom narratives or archetypal story formation. It is what our psyches do with the unprocessed cultural dynamics emerging at the level of unconscious functioning.

This interpenetration and overlapping of Black/white psyches in America around race is part of the legacy (intergenerationally) that we have inherited as part of our American citizenship – its contradictions, conflicts, and shadows. Historically, these overlapping forces have been imagined in different ways, but seem to always include the issues of namelessness, invisibility, marginalization, and domination for Black people.

Another description of archetypal bonding can be seen in W. E. B. Dubois's work from over a century ago. Dubois used the metaphor of the color line to identify how racial complexes divide and work out differences through domination, imposition of values, attitudes, ideology, and institutionalization. Using current psychoanalytic language, these processes contribute to the production of collective projective processes that work to collapse cultural spaces. These dynamics undercut relating, by turning persons into objects through depersonalization and dehumanization. These are processes that collapse transitional space, foreclosing meaning.

Toni Morrison, in her book of essays *Playing in the Dark* (1993), offers a way of imagining this racialized intersubjective space through looking at the way the Africanist presence is represented in American literature. She points to the prevalent themes in nineteenth-century literature that are based on a "pressing toward a human freedom, a kind of human dignity believed to be unprecedented . . . collapsed into the phrase 'The American Dream'" (Morrison, 1993, p. 33).

This American Dream had bounded up within it

> "blank darkness," to conveniently bound and violently silenced black bodies. . . . Black slavery enriched the country's creative possibilities. For in that construction of blackness and enslavement could be found not only the not-free but also, with the dramatic polarity created by skin color, the projection of the not-me. . . . What rose up out of collective needs to ally internal fears and to rationalize external exploitation was an American Africanism – a fabricated brew of darkness, otherness, alarm, and desire that is uniquely American.
>
> (p. 38)

Morrison is describing how unconscious collective projections are built into our cultural setup at the fantasy level. This setup evokes racialized fantasies that contribute to the organization of anxiety around race and differences. These fantasies express the organization of the individual's and group's intersubjective experiences of differences. Coates and Baldwin in their letters to their son and nephew, respectively, and Morrison in her essay all converge around the recognition that blackness was a construction of whiteness but that whiteness being assumed to be universal and "given" was also a construction that came along with privileges and power (see DiAngelo, 2018).

As elucidated in Chapter 4, Jung defines projection as an intentional, unconscious transfer of subjective aspects into the other (1971, para. 783). In this sense the projector defends themselves against anything new that might alter the projection. We don't always see what we are participating in nor what we are creating. The movie *Get Out* shows the horrific process of turning the other into an object through splitting, which not only alienates danger and destructiveness into others, but also uses the warmth and vitality of the other to appropriate humanity and feeling into a deadened and empty life. Treating a person of color as a fetish, in other words, can be used to export degradation and to import passion and energy. The issues in *Get Out* are the typical ones of Black invisibility, namelessness, and social and civic death that are denied visibility and the freedom to articulate their own spiritual strivings (see West, 2013; Patterson, 1982). Shortly after seeing the movie, I had the following dream, which helped me to see what I was not quite seeing.

> *I am on a college campus in an older building when I come across a number of people milling around what looks like a classroom. I look inside and folks are putting chairs in a circle and I then realize that I am expected to lead group process training. I'm surprised, as I do not remember planning or agreeing to participate in such an event. I vaguely recognize some of the participants as colleagues and even patients. As I accept the fact that I am leading, the dream changes and now I am with a small group of older, white, professional-looking people. A feeling of dis-ease comes over me and I, spontaneously, ask them to show me their teeth in the way I am baring mine (as if I am going to bite something or attack). They do, and they have wolf teeth.*

I awoke in a state of shock (in the dream as well as out of the dream) as I realized that I was seeing directly into the unconscious of this group of people.

Fairy tales and mythology describe the wolf as being associated with the gods Apollo, Wotan, Mars, the devil, and even with the feminine principal. We associate to the hungry wolf, the lone wolf, that indiscriminate desire "to eat up everybody and everything, to have everything i.e., greed – they're never satisfied. *Homo homini lupus*, Man is a wolf to man" (Peskin, 2012). What is feared in the other turns out to contribute to our own dehumanization. "What is feared . . . is not physical extinction but loss of humanness: a psychological death . . . in which our humanness would permanently come to an end (Kohut, 1971,

p. 16) – that aspect of us that loses contact with our humanness. Unlike little Max in *Where the Wild Things Are*, we rarely realize that we are in the midst of a projection-making process that turns the other into an object. We lose the other as subject, the person of the other. We become wolves. What can we do?

Morrison shows us that the best way of transforming objects into subjects, to real people, is to let the voiceless and the invisible ones express their own interiorities in their own language, words, and through their own experiences.

Recently there has been an emergent focus on the deconstruction of whiteness to make whiteness transparent. To confront unexamined assumptions, to see whiteness as a social construction, as an unmarked category that accrues power and domination, is the new task. Today there is some recognition of the emotional issues around whiteness and the impact of racism on the white psyche. These are some of the areas being studied:

- Inclusion and exclusion
- Post Traumatic Slavery Syndrome
- White rage
- White privilege
- White fragility
- Implicit bias
- Microaggression

To briefly summarize the implications of the research and work being done in the aforementioned areas: the focus is on identifying and recognizing both the overt structures that define white privilege and disproportionately put people of color at a disadvantage in areas of housing, healthcare and access, criminal justice system outcomes, wealth and income while covering up the harm that those privileges provide. In other words, the rewards of privilege as an unconsciousness dynamic is dissociated, repressed, or covered by the power dynamics of domination and subjugation as well as the history that such processes have generated in pain and anguish for people of color over the centuries. This work is focused on unveiling the white racial complex, acknowledging it, and ultimately (for whites) mourning it.

We have to not only look at individual fantasy but also read the collective, historically contingent fantasies carried in the group and in the individual. We must earn to read the traces of an experience's impact on subjectivity – the effects of something, not the thing itself, a kind of shadow across the unconscious – the long shadow of slavery as it impacts the lives of everyday people. This is a type of haunting; this is where the wild things live:

> It is an animated state in which a repressed or unresolved social violence is making itself known, sometimes very directly, sometimes more obliquely . . . a presence that demands its due, your attention. . . . Haunting raises specters, and it alters the experience of being in linear time, alters the way we normally separate and sequence the past, the present, and the future. These specters or ghosts appear when the trouble they represent and symptomize is no longer being contained or repressed or blocked from view. The ghost, as I understand it, is not the invisible or some ineffable excess. The whole essence, if you can use that word, of a ghost is that it has a real presence and demands its due, demands your attention.
>
> (Gordon, 2008, p. xvi)

Our relationships around race in the United States, especially for whites and people of color, are haunted by all manner of unacknowledged specters. Whiteness is a fabricated brew of darkness – otherness, alarm, and desire (Morrison, 1993). To return to our hero Max, through his secure attachment, he is able to play with the terrible, frightening aspects of reality wearing his wolf clothes. In racialized relating, the real is too real to play with – it is a serious and deadly business.

References

Baldwin, J. (1963). The day my dungeon shook. In *The fire next time*. New York, NY: Dial Press.

Benjamin, J. (1995). *Like subjects, love objects: Essays on recognition*. New Haven, CT: Yale University Press.

Coates, T.-N. (2015). *Between the world and me*. New York, NY: Penguin Random House.

DiAngelo, R. (2018). *White fragility: Why it's so hard for white people to talk about race*. Boston, MA: Beacon Press.

Dourley, J. (2003). Archetypal hatred as social bond: Strategies for its dissolution, in terror, violence and the impulse to destroy. In J. Beebe (Ed.), *Terror, violence, and the impulse to destroy*. Einsiedeln, Switzerland: Daimon Verlag.

Du Bois, W. E. B. (1903/2003). *The soul of Black folks*. New York, NY: New American Library.

Gordon, A. F. (2008). *Ghostly matters: Haunting and the sociological imagination*. Minneapolis, MN: University of Minnesota Press.

Jung, C. G. (1971). *Psychological types*. Princeton, NJ: Princeton University Press.

Kohut, H. (1971). *The analysis of the self: A systematic approach to the psychoanalytic treatment of narcissistic personality disorders*. New York, NY: International Universities Press.

Morrison, T. (1993). *Playing in the dark: Whiteness and the literary imagination*. New York, NY: Vintage Books.

Patterson, O. (1982). *Slavery and social death: A comparative study*. Cambridge, MA: Harvard University Press.

Peskin, H. (2012). Man is a wolf to man: Issues of dehumanization in psychoanalysis. *Psychoanalytic Dialogues, 22*(2), 190–205.

Sendak, M. (1963). *Where the wild things are*. New York, NY: HarperCollins.

West, C. (2013, June–August). On Black strivings. *The Brotherwise Dispatch, 2*(8). Retrieved from http://brotherwisedispatch.blogspot.com/2013/06/on-black-strivings-by-cornel-west.html

Winnicott, D. W. (1971). *Playing and reality*. London: Routledge.

Chapter 7

A framework for cultural activism in the consulting room

> . . . the long line of forever stretches into the future and the last night
> of the universe is already suspect and falling . . .
>
> August Wilson (1992)

This chapter offers a way to think about and to work with cultural phantoms, the phantom narratives that become active presences in cultures and in our analytic work. My hope is this approach to narrative truth will begin to open up psychic spaces for thinking about and working with some of the most painful and intractable aspects of our psychocultural life.

The topic of analysis and social activism brings together opposites in the way we typically conceive of our analytic field. There are obvious issues around the analytic frame of neutrality, the use of internal constructs, and the transference/countertransference with their emphasis on the dyadic, witnessing versus detachment, privileged apartness versus active participation, or, as Peskin indicated, how therapeutic neutrality is to psychic reality as witnessing is to the recovery of social reality (2012, p. 2). I have found that wrestling with these issues, while sitting in my office at the crossroads where individuality and culture meet, can be a challenge to generating for my clients an intersubjective space that releases the potential for humanizing the contact around differences, and for processing our mutual messiness when cultural complexes are activated and society enters the treatment room, filling the space with the hope for social change. Though we might put cultural issues of class, race, gender, and ethnicity in the background, every word, gesture, and indeed the very structure that we set up and participate in exude a cultural stance. We are always in the cultural unconscious. To paraphrase Bromberg, the really real are not just fantasies but real events that shape our psyches and their processes (2001, pp. 385–386).

We become awake or conscious out of the cultural unconscious from which we are born, through the contemplation of signs, signifiers, and symbols that antedate us. We become conscious of what life means to us, that is, in a world already ripe with meaning. Thus dissociating the individual patient from that person's cultural background distances us from what our patient is struggling to construe. An analyst then risks becoming a voyeur or a bystander, masquerading as an objective observer. As Bodnar says, "Interpretations, enactments, and the relationship construction unconsciously replicate unexamined tenets of the analyst's cultural beliefs" (2004, p. 581). Not to become aware of the interpenetration of psyche and cultural factors within the analytic context may turn the analysis into a scene for the enactment of cultural history where the intergenerational transmission of personal and cultural trauma will meet once again within a nuclear family, this time a dyadically configured unconscious, shielding the pair who are actually repeating cultural history from the larger social world they would have otherwise wanted to transform. The ongoing difficulties of bridging some of the tensions of culture and psyche are made more complicated when these make their appearance simply as anxiety around differences and when they are expressed as acted-out cultural complexes.

Slavoj Žižek, Slovenian social theorist and psychoanalyst, related a parable about the ignorance of a chicken, and it speaks to the inextricable bind we find ourselves in when we try too quickly to rectify a culturally replicative clinical course by bringing culture and psyche, activism and analysis together. As Žižek's (2005) story goes, a man finds himself admitted to a mental hospital because he believes himself to be a piece of grain. Working with his mental health team within the hospital, he comes to accept that he is not what he fears and seems to have conquered his delusion and is therefore released from the hospital. Shortly after his departure, he comes running back to the hospital and reports to the staff that upon leaving the hospital he came upon a chicken and had a panic attack. His doctor reassures the patient that he has nothing to worry about, for he is not something to be eaten, so not to worry about the chicken. The patient responds, "I know I am not a piece of grain, and you know I'm not a piece of grain, but I am not so sure that the chicken knows that I'm not a piece of grain."

In responding to this story, Prager makes the point not only do benign objects get transformed into terrifying ones but also "the parable captures the limits of therapeutic cure" – the close system of the dyadic relationship (2011, p. 426). The (analytic) pair can become its own closed system as bulwark against the world. I believe many analysts are now trying to think about how to open up the pair and include the world with all its ambiguities and messiness.

On a larger scale, cultural themes in our globalized world inevitably express forms, figures, and presences that carry the fears, hopes, and identity needs derived from breakdown in the traditions and disruptions in continuity of our life processes. The role of analytical psychology in cultural and political affairs is to help elaborate our understanding of, and relationship to, intersubjective forms that actually represent cultural complexes. These masquerading forms are cultural phantoms, and I invite the reader to observe how they play themselves out in psychological and cultural life. Cultural complexes and projective defenses (often appearing as strikingly revenant images) are powerful players in the generation of phantom narratives that offer themselves, once again, as a counterpoint to received notions of progress in history and social policy. These narratives are the expressions of marginalized, invisible stories that surprisingly often haunt the analytic narrative. They express drives toward the need for recognition and urges against death and annihilation, and they are regularly expressed in social structures and policies that produce non-recognition. Among those are analysis and how analysis is taught.

In what is therefore a moral crisis for the analytic field, the question is how to transform collective processes when they enter the consulting room or the training institution. Toward this end we might want to understand our own group process in a way that facilitates greater consciousness. We can contribute to a training group's development when we learn to recognize and work with presences in the collective unconscious and of the unconscious in the collective that are unprocessed cultural phantoms. Behind cultural attitudes and expressions of cultural complexes, cultural phantoms often manifest the absences of marginalized history – the many collective histories from genocide, the Holocaust, and slavery to the everyday presences of the cultural backgrounds of analysts and patients that manifest the very same power disparities and racial hierarchies that are found in the culture.

Fortunately, racial and ethnic identity formation are not only shaped by internalized negative cultural attitudes toward a particular racial, ethnic, or gender group but also by the positive contribution that one's cultural group contributes to identity formation.

In *Lament of the Dead*, Shamdasani and Hillman, through their long conversation stimulated by Jung's *Red Book*, constantly return to a theme that relates human cultural ancestry, the weight of human history, with the paradox that the dead "present themselves as figures of a historic moment, or of a historic period at least, but they're not historic figures" (2013, p. 3). This theme relates to my notion of cultural phantoms and their relationship to politics and social life. Just as the spirits of the dead are, as Jung says, "voices of the Unanswered, Unresolved, and Unredeemed" (1989, p. 191), cultural phantoms are expressions of our unevolved collective imaginary, "haunted" by phantoms of specifically stuck historical events (traumas) that then get passed along to later generations and organized in politics, social forms, rituals, and relationships that turn on inclusions and exclusions and repressive and dissociative power dynamics. Cultural phantoms are images (formations) of cultural complexes that link individual valence with group narrative.

To encounter such hungry ghosts in the background of analysis, the psychopolitical terms we too often summon to explain them away must find a way to break with the comforting linear chronology of history we call "progress" and look beneath the received history of developing consciousness toward another narrative that makes room for stuckness and repetition of unsolved cultural issues. The narrative we need to uncover in our work is the phantom narrative, one which calls into question the official narrative of the evolution of consciousness that many analysts live in and take for granted, because it authorizes analysis to succeed without having to look at all it has been leaving out. To reflect on phantom narratives, and let in other perspectives than the accepted ones, brings competing interpretations into play and opens questions, conflicts, and wounds that cannot be so easily closed in the name of healing. To paraphrase Avery Gordon, the continued presence of the cultural unconscious in relationship to unacknowledged violence is haunting. "What's distinctive about haunting is that it is an animated state in which a repressed or unresolved social violence is making itself known" – sometimes as repetitive instances when home becomes unfamiliar, when your bearings on the world lose direction, when the over-and-done-with comes alive, when what's been in your blind spot comes into view (2008, xvi).

Phantom narratives call into question a future based on taking care of past grievances, harms, and traumas by transcending them; they bid we open the mouths of the dead (as in Jung's *Red Book*) to see what still needs to be voiced. Cultural phantoms call into question the modern stories we tell ourselves about how things have become, which so often delude as to the way things really are. Descriptions of past historical events, escaping from the mouths of the dead, represent the persisting damage done. They haunt us with the memory of missed historical alternatives. These phantomatic presences richly conjure, describe, narrate, and inform and thus they begin to explain to us the costs, the forfeits, and the abusive powers that have also shaped us in the name of progress.

Nor are phantom narratives simply "the return of the repressed" and therefore "the past." The future haunts us too, in the name of the present, in the spirit of being millennially "with it." Simultaneity, multiplicity, virtuality, new media, and digital technology are also specters, ways of describing our world that attempt to transcend distinctions like inner/outer, subject/object, and the immaterial/material only to bring forth new traumas, dilemmas, and phantoms for future generations to struggle with. We, as was Jung a hundred years ago when his worst private fears were confirmed in the history emerging around him, are at a theoretical crossroad. We are being born into a new myth of collective consciousness, and we are learning that this is still what Henderson was the first to call the cultural unconscious. These days, I think of the cultural unconscious as having a spectral quality. As Derrida puns, ontology and hauntology have flipped, and the spectral has taken precedence over the fantasy of cultural ontology. The familiar, with its past, has become the unfamiliar with its future: marginalization, alienation, homelessness, and existential anxiety at a level the existentialists never imagined. These have become the familiar context, not just for our being, but for our becoming, and form a specter that haunts the future of individuation in our consulting rooms.

The phantom, as image, arose as an expression of historical memory, one that conveys a kind of living continuity between past and present. It has always, ontologically, been an internal, not external, history that brings "something prior to history" (Corbin, 1980). This inner history, as Murray Stein states, "is the story of meaning, in which time and eternity, consciousness and unconsciousness, specific historical and archetypal forces all together perform their roles and produce a particular configuration in time" (2014, p. 111), and, I would add, particular representations.

But it is now a proto-narrative too, heralding the uncertainties of the future. Living internal memories create a cultural symbolic space in which memories and events are held, elaborated, and come to signify the spirit of the group that will shape many things still to come. This living spirit becomes a rolling zeitgeist – the spirit of a particular historical time and place continually becoming incorporated as part of the group and individual's identity, not just now, but as its future as well. Jung's reflections on this shocking conservative level of the group psyche are present in his use of Levy-Bruhl's term *participation mystique*, referring to that level of group functioning in which we conserve the nature of culture by acting and reacting, thinking and feeling like others in the group in a way that challenges any possibility of genuine individuation. This level of archaic identity can evolve into symbolic images that designate the ongoing "presence of the absence" of a piece of transgenerational narrative. Through this, marginalized or dissociated psychic states can be represented as phantoms with a frightening future.

But I would point out that there is hope in knowing this. August Wilson (1992), the great African American playwright, has said it best:

There are always and only two trains running. There is life and there is death. Each of us rides them both. To live life with dignity, to celebrate and accept responsibility for your presence in the world is all that can be asked of anyone.

References

Bodnar, S. (2004). Remember where you come from: Dissociative process in multicultural individuals. *Psychoanalytic Dialogues*, *14*(5), 581–603.
Bromberg, P. (2001). The gorilla did it: Some thoughts on dissociation, the real, and the really real. *Psychoanalytic Dialogues*, *11*(3), 385–404.
Corbin, J. (1980). *The question of comparative philosophy*. Dallas, TX: Spring Publications.
Gordon, A. F. (2008). *Ghostly matters: Haunting and the sociological imagination*. Minneapolis, MN: University of Minnesota Press.
Jung, C. G. (1989). *Memories, dreams, reflections*. New York, NY: Vintage.
Peskin, H. (2012). Man is a wolf to man: Issues of dehumanization in psychoanalysis. *Psychoanalytic Dialogues*, *22*(2), 190–205.
Prager, J. (2011). Danger and deformation: A social theory of trauma Part 1. *American Imago*, *68*(3), 425–448.
Shamdasani, S., & Hillman, J. (2013). *Lament of the dead: Psychology after Jung's Red Book*. New York, NY: W.W. Norton & Company.
Stein, M. (2014). *Practicing wholeness*. Asheville, NC: Chiron.
Wilson, A. (1992). Foreword to *Two trains running*. New York, NY: Plume/Penguin.
Žižek, S. (2005, November 18). *The ignorance of chicken*. Presentation for the New School for Social Research.

Chapter 8

James Baldwin and Toni Morrison

Othering through racialized intersubjectivities

Over the decades many have found the literary works of James Baldwin and Toni Morrison to have ongoing relevance to the social and psychological issues of our times. Whether we are confronting issues of immigration, gender, Black Lives Matter, healthcare inequalities, or injustice, their reflections provide ways to hold, understand, and process what is happening on the sociopolitical stage as well as in our inner psychic landscape by igniting transformative processes that are relevant to current times. Their writings share with psychoanalysis the use of language as a way to open subtle levels of lived experience, sharing and participating in the personal and cultural contexts that are expressions of the life of the psyche. In this chapter, I look at their works through the lens of analytical psychology and, specifically, the concepts of the cultural complex and phantom narratives, which offer us a way to link analytical psychology with literary expression.

James Baldwin (August 2, 1924) and Toni Morrison (February 28, 1931) were born seven years apart. They had a profound impact not only on each other but also, by extension, on the rest of us, Black and white people alike, in terms of how they opened up racialized cultural complexes for examination and thereby helped in both their and our transformations. Their medium was literature, which served as a vehicle for processing their (and our) experiences of racism. In this chapter I focus on two aspects that both authors brought to our attention that help us reflect on othering:

- The transformation of their relationship to each other through the shared attitudes toward the cultural complex of racialized intersubjectivity.
- Their relationship to their inner life as a source of strength and the foundation for an imagination that allowed them to hold the love and destruction that they found around them.

In their writings, Baldwin and Morrison describe an intricate psychosocial, political fabric around race relations, its constructions, functions, and representations in American society from slavery to the Jim Crow era to the Civil Rights Movement up to and including the present day. Baldwin is most associated with the late 1950s and 1960s, when during these historical times the cultural focus around race relations was on resistance and protest; Morrison is often seen through the eyes of gender and feminism. But beginning with her first book (*The Bluest Eyes*, 1970) and continuing to the last (*The Source of Self-Regard*, 2019), the works she created put the African American experience at the center.

Both Baldwin and Morrison focus on the construction in language of literary representations of African American experiences, pointing to a psychological framework for working with the negative effects produced by the conscious and unconscious racist attitudes that define Black people as other. They also expose how unexamined but privileged whiteness provides a taken-for-granted normative context that covers and shadows attitudes about power and exclusion. Examining issues around intraracial self-hatred, racialized projections, introjections, and projective identifications as psychological mechanisms, they help us see how racial violence lives deeply within both victims and perpetrators.

I use the phrase *racialized intersubjectivities* to frame the collapse of the relational space of mutual recognitions (similar to Benjamin's "like subjects" with their separate but related attitudes (1995)). This collapsed space is generated by intergenerational, unprocessed histories of genocidal violence and socio-emotional political situations created around dominance and subjugation, inclusion and exclusion. These unprocessed situations contribute to the creation of racialized subjects whose own identity and subjectivity have also been shaped by these forces. Ogden (2004) writes about the "subjugated third" to refer to the "jointly created unconscious, but collapsed space in the analytic pair," I expand the term to describe the unconsciously created racialized intersubjectivities that carry the history of racism, racial violence, and privilege, including that of denial. The psychological work done around this mutually created situation requires, at a minimum, recognition and acknowledgment of our contribution to this racialized intersubjectivity, that is, myself as subject and as object, others as both "them" and "like us."

Both Morrison and Baldwin looked at the cultural attitudes that supported the creation of otherness, even as they themselves struggled at times to deal with feelings of being the marginalized other in society. Both explored the psychological effects of racism on the victims of such violence as well as the effects on whites as perpetrators of such violence and fear toward people of color, shining a light on the role of silence and denial of unacknowledged conscious and unconscious violence. In *Playing in the Dark: Whiteness and the Literary Imagination*, Morrison states,

> My early assumptions . . . were black people signified nothing in the imagination of white American writers. Other than as the objects of an occasional bout of jungle fever, other than to provide color or to lend some touch of verisimilitude or to supply a needed moral gesture, humor, or bit of pathos, blacks made no appearance at all.
>
> (1992, p. 15)

Winnicott's concept of the use of an object helps me to elaborate Morrison's and Baldwin's work. This is helpful especially when looking at our collective failure to discover our social use of others as dehumanized objects/others (such as Black characters in white literature) where Blacks are marginalized and denigrated objects used for the normalization of the white gaze that objectifies and dehumanizes.

> When I speak of the use of an object, . . . I take object-relating for granted, and add new features that involve the nature and the behavior of the object. For instance, the object, if it is to be used, must necessarily be real in the sense of being part of shared reality, not a bundle of projections.
>
> (Winnicott, 1969, p. 711)

A bundle of projections that, as Montagu says, defines "Race [as] the witchcraft of our time; the means by which we exorcise demons. It is the contemporary myth. Man's most dangerous myth" (1942, p. 41).

It is in their attempts to talk and write about these complicated, racialized subjectivities that Baldwin and Morrison repeatedly overlap:

> The long list of parallels between Morrison's and Baldwin's writing styles and traditional black forms of artistic expression, include. . . . The rhythms that recall the tam-tam drums of African tribes, slave work songs, black sermons, and contemporary rap music. The other stories hidden behind the base plot, the (inter)play of multiple meanings, and the frequent biblical allusions (Moses, Bridegroom, Lord, and Bethlehem in Baldwin; apple, Eve, Adam, and paradise in Morrison) remind us of the coded language of slaves, and of gospels and spirituals.
>
> (Kerchy, 2006, p. 43)

The transformation of Black subjectivity refers to the movement from being objects to becoming subjects. Through my perspective as an African American psychologist and Jungian analyst, I have similarly studied and explored the aforementioned dynamics throughout my professional life and analytic work. Looking through the lens of racialized intersubjectivities provides a way to reflect on how chronic polarizations about race have and continue to provoke unconscious processes, which I named *phantom narratives*, as carriers (expressions) of cultural complexes (Kimbles, 2014). I feel Jung had a similar understanding when he stated,

> Below the threshold of consciousness, the contagion meets with little resistance. Just as the coloured man lives in your cities and even within your houses, so also he lives under your skin, subconsciously. Naturally it works both ways. Just as every Jew has a Christ complex, so every Negro has a white complex and every American a Negro complex.
>
> (1968a, CW 10, para. 963)

These processes are very much alive in the works of Morrison and Baldwin where they write about the vibrant traumatic shadows of our unprocessed experience, our unacknowledged histories around differences in gender, race, and inclusion and exclusion. I have found that engaging these issues through literature and analytical psychology can ignite transformative processes in both the individual psyche as well as the cultural psyche.

Both Morrison and Baldwin saw the other's work as transformative in its effects on them. In a 1989 book of eulogies in remembrance of Baldwin, Morrison says of Baldwin:

> You gave me a language to dwell in, a gift so perfect it seems my own invention. I have been thinking your spoken and written thoughts for so long I believed they were mine. I have been seeing the world through your eyes for so long, I believe that clear, clear view was my own.
>
> (Troupe, 1989, p. 76)

Morrison and Baldwin's approach to writing and literature generated a way of looking at and understanding racialized intersubjectivities both within our culture and ourselves. By *racialized intersubjectivities*, I am referring to that intersubjective space that is structured (mostly unconsciously) by the traumas and violence connected with racial suffering.

This suffering grows out of our particular cultural, social historical realities, which provide context for many of the signs and symptoms of individual suffering that we frequently see in our consulting rooms. These processes manifest in miscommunications that make having discussions around race and differences difficult, often leading to misperceptions of private and social pain (DiAngelo, 2018).

Collective suffering is structured by cultural complexes that make visible emotional forces that operate implicitly in two areas: intergenerational process and expressions of collective shadow processes. These implicit structures and forces are *phantom narratives*, the archetypal stories of the presence-absence of emotional forces in our social and political lives. To quote Jung, "these processes are 'psychically charged and volatile.'" "Our fearsome gods, have only changed their names: they now rhyme with -ism" (1969, CW 7, para. 326), "for the true historical event lies deeply buried, experienced by all and observed by none. It is the most private and most subjective of psychic experiences" (1968b, CW 10, para. 315). I don't think it is an overstatement when I say that Baldwin's and Morrison's works are amplifications of Jung's description of unconscious social processes in their own words.

An example of the expression of racialized intersubjectivities appeared in a recent *New York Times* Op Ed piece by Charles Blow (2019), titled "Trumpism's Infinite Vulgarities":

> Trump went on more profanity laced tirades. At a campaign rally in Minnesota Trump said of Joe Biden: "He was only a good vice president because he understood how to kiss Barack Obama's ass."
>
> Let's ignore for the moment that one could not find a more obsequious vice president than Mike Pence, a man who looks at Trump like he's made of rainbows and cotton candy.
>
> Let's instead focus on the coding of the charge against Biden, whether Trump is conscious of it or not, whether it was intentional or not.
>
> The insult invokes a fear and disdain that white racists have had throughout American history: The subjugation of the white man to the black man. Indeed, Jim Crow was born out of a fear of "Negro domination" in which white Southerners were deadly afraid that they could be forced to live under black rule in the wake of the Civil War.

This racially coded language is an example of what I call the *primal scene layer* of the psyche that seems always available to be activated (racialized complexes) when something or someone acts and speaks to and from that level of confusion and fear around social differences.

I never met Baldwin or Morrison, but as a teen I had an experience of Baldwin, the effects of which I still feel deeply today. I grew up in Jackson, Mississippi, for the first ten years of my life. My parents divorced, and I, along with my siblings, moved to Los Angeles to be with my mother's family. After a couple of years in Los Angeles, I had enough of feeling alienated from the Black community, and, besides, Los Angeles never felt contained or holding the way Jackson did. I decided on my own to return to Jackson. A number of transformative things happened, including being exposed to Baldwin, who came to my high school to speak at a school assembly. I remembered him being introduced, stepping up to the podium, looking slowly over the sea of young Black adolescent teens. After this long silence, he said, "Remember boys and girls, if you bang your heads against a book and you hear an empty sound, never think that the sound is coming from your heads first. The book may not be speaking to you." I interpret Baldwin as saying, the author may not have had you in mind (your own lived experience) as the audience. I felt an enormous sense of inner space, which I have come to cherish.

Both Baldwin and Morrison wrote about that quality of inner space that served as a foundation for all their literary work and the ground of their being. In the following quotes I let Baldwin and Morrison themselves speak about and from the ground of their own being:

> Perhaps the primary distinction of the artist is that he must actively cultivate that state which most men, necessarily, must avoid: the state of being alone. That all men are, when the chips are down, alone, is a banality – a banality because it is very frequently stated, but very rarely, on the evidence, believed. The precise role of the artist, then, is to illuminate that darkness, blaze roads through that vast forest, so that we will not, in all our doing, lose sight of its purpose, which is, after all, to make the world a more human dwelling place.
>
> (Baldwin, 1962, p. 1)

Here Baldwin identifies that our deep attention to our interiority provides the foundation for the grounding of our subjective experiences in a racialized cultural context.

In an essay on *Blavity*, rdmeeks explores Toni Morrison's focus on rootedness:

> As we move through the world, I hope that our relationship to it is not defined by things outside ourselves. Our ancestral lands and people are within us. Baby Suggs, in *Beloved*, taught us that "definitions belong to the definers," and the message of this essay calls us to define ourselves, as we want, on solid ground.
>
> (rdmeeks, 2018)

In "Rootedness: The Ancestor as Foundation," Morrison paid deep attention to the intergenerational aspects of racialized attitudes. Consider the following comments:

> What struck me in looking at some contemporary fiction was that whether the novel took place in the city or in the country the presence or absence of that figure [the ancestor] determined the success or the happiness of the character. It was the absence of an ancestor that was frightening, that was threatening, it caused huge destruction and disarray in the work itself.
>
> (Morrison, quoted in rdmeeks, 2018)

We can hear Morrison's words through the lens of an intergenerational orientation. Another powerful example of her imagination is expressed in the essay "The Slavebody and the Blackbody." After reviewing the growth of America's economy using slave labor, she says:

> That is what must be remembered. There is another power this project has: of making us aware of the ever flexible, always adaptable, persistently slippery forms of modern racism in which the slavebody is reconstructed and reenters the blackbody as an American form of ethnic cleansing in which a monstrously large number of black men and women are carefully swept into prisons, they become once again free labor; once again corralled for profit.
>
> (2019, p. 77)

One of Morrison's greatest contributions to literature was the wide and deep vision with which she saw Black people – her deep compassion, her characters' deep, complex interiority. In that deep seeing, she reverses the representation and positions of white people, putting them into the position of the other. This allowed her to focus on Blacks as subjects while forcing whites to experience themselves as the other. The otherness of whites refers to white denial of their ongoing (unconscious) relationship with historical slavery and present-day social inequality and injustice. Again, quoting Baldwin (1961, p. 217): "The thing that most white people imagine they can salvage from the storm of life is really, in sum, their innocence." Hence, confronting the denial and historical amnesia connected to the perpetuation of entrenched racism is the focus of both Morrison and Baldwin (the racialized cultural complex), although they approached these racialized complexes from different attitudes. Baldwin used an extroverted, confrontative approach, calling out our hypocrisies and challenging destructive racial projections (I highly recommend the documentary *I Am Not Your Negro*). Morrison approached these same forces by speaking through a deeply introverted attitude that sought out the exposure of the deleterious effects of racism on the humanity of the victims as she tells their stories. She believed in the power of literature – as a social good was deeply expressed in all her writings. In a 2015 essay for *The Nation*, "No Place for Self Pity, No Room for Fear," she wrote,

> I know the world is bruised and bleeding, and though it is important not to ignore its pain, it is also critical to refuse to succumb to its malevolence. Like failure, chaos contains information that can lead to knowledge – even wisdom.
>
> (p. 1)

Through their writings both Baldwin and Morrison are able to stimulate psychic and emotional processes, which have the power to transform our relationships to ingrained racial structures by stimulating our own identification, recognition, and imagination on how these processes live within and without us. We may recognize the rupture that has happened in our personal and social lives, as racism has impacted us all. Again, I quote Morrison: "There is no time for despair, no place for self-pity, no need for silence, no room for fear. We speak, we write, we do language. That is how civilizations heal" (2015, p. 1).

In a recent book, *The Implicated Subject*, Michael Rothberg says the following:

> Implicated subjects occupy positions aligned with power and privilege without being themselves direct agents of harm; they contribute to, inhabit, inherit, or benefit from regimes of domination but do not originate or control such regimes. An implicated subject is neither a victim nor perpetrator, but rather a participant in histories and social formations that generate the positions of victim and perpetrator.
>
> (2019, p. 1)

Baldwin's and Morrison's work also has clinical implications:

A racialized subjectivity is usually carried by those with darker skin colors, whereas whiteness is experienced as an unmarked and invisible state. Whites have dissociated the historical position of the oppressor from collective consciousness, due to our inability to tolerate identification with the aggressor. Our disavowal of race as constitutive of subjectivity ensures that race becomes a site for enactments.

(Suchet, 2004, p. 423)

Racial, social, and class issues tend to be silent in the background of whatever clinical work we are doing. These large group dynamics are rarely looked at as contributions to the development of our subjectivity and our psychic situation. Hence, in psychotherapy and analysis, transference/countertransference dynamics at times enact unrecognized cultural realities which are "the distinctive configurations of self and other that shape and organize a person's subjective world" (Atwood & Stolorow, 2014, p. 28). As an example, the trauma of slavery and its continued contribution to cultural violence, social injustice, and income inequalities provide a primal context for our work.

We are all implicated subjects in this "psychically charged and volatile" work, which brings up unavoidable ethical and moral implications for us.

References

Atwood, G., & Stolorow, R. (2014). *Structures of subjectivity*. London and New York, NY: Routledge.

Baldwin, J. (1961). The black boy looks at the white boy. In *Nobody knows my name: More notes of a native son*. New York, NY: Dial Press.

Baldwin, J. (1962). The creative process. In *Creative America*. New York, NY: Ridge Press.

Benjamin, J. (1995). *Like subjects, love objects: Essays on recognition and sexual differences*. New Haven, CT: Yale University Press.

Blow, C. (2019, October 13). Trumpism's infinite vulgarities. *New York Times*. Retrieved from www.nytimes.com/2019/10/13/opinion/trump-republicans. html

DiAngelo, R. (2018). *White fragility: Why it's so hard for white people to talk about race*. Boston, MA: Beacon Press.

Jung, C. G. (1968a). The complications of American psychology (1930). In *The collected works of C.G. Jung: Vol. 10. Civilization in transition*. Princeton, NJ: Princeton University Press.

Jung, C. G. (1968b). The meaning of psychology for modern man (1934). In *The collected works of C.G. Jung: Vol. 10. Civilization in transition*. Princeton, NJ: Princeton University Press.

Jung, C. G. (1969). The relations between the ego and the unconscious (1928). In *The collected works of C.G. Jung: Vol. 7. Two essays on analytical psychology*. Princeton, NJ: Princeton University Press.

Kerchy, A. (2006). Narrating the beat of the heart, jazzing the text of desire: A comparative interface of James Baldwin's *Another Country* and Toni Morrison's *Jazz*. In L. King & L. O. Scott (Eds.), *James Baldwin and Toni Morrison: Comparative critical and theoretical essays* (pp. 37–62). New York, NY: MacMillan.

Kimbles, S. (2014). *Phantom narratives: The unseen contributions of culture to psyche*. Lanham, MD: Rowman and Littlefield.

Montagu, A. (1942). *Man's most dangerous myth*. Lanham, MD: Rowman & Littlefield.

Morrison, T. (1970). *The bluest eye*. New York, NY: Holt, Rinehart and Winston.

Morrison, T. (1992). *Playing in the dark: Whiteness and the literary imagination*. Cambridge, MA: Harvard University Press.

Morrison, T. (2015, March 13). No place for self-pity, no room for fear. *The Nation*. Retrieved from www.thenation.com/article/archive/no-place-self-pity-no-room-fear/

Morrison, T. (2019). *The source of self-regard*. New York, NY: Vintage Books.

Ogden, T. H. (2004). The analytic third: Implications for psychoanalytic theory and technique. *Psychoanalytic Quarterly, 73*(1), 167–195.

rdmeeks. (2018, February 2). How Toni Morrison focused on "rootedness" and 5 other authors who followed suit. *Blavity News*. Retrieved from https://blavity.com/how-toni-morrison-focused-on-rootedness-and-other-authors-who-followed-suit?category1=blavityreads&subCat=community-submitted

Rothberg, M. (2019). *The implicated subject: Beyond victims and perpetrators*. Stanford, CA: Stanford University Press.

Suchet, M. (2004). A relational encounter with race. *Psychoanalytic Dialogues, 14*, 422–438.

Troupe, Q. (Ed.). (1989). *James Baldwin: The legacy*. New York, NY: Simon & Schuster.

Winnicott, D. W. (1969). The use of an object. *International Journal of Psychoanalysis, 50*, 711–716.

Index